MEN SURVIVING INCEST

MEN SURVIVING INCEST

A Male Survivor Shares on the Process of Recovery

by   T. THOMAS

LAUNCH PRESS

Walnut Creek, California

Printed in the United States of America

97 96 95 94 93 92 91 90   5 4 3 2 1

Library of Congress Cataloging in Publication Data

Thomas, T.,   1955-
    Men surviving incest: a male survivor shares on the
    process of recovery / by T. Thomas.
        p.   cm.
    Includes bibliographical references.
    ISBN 0-9613205-8-3   : $7.95
    1. Adult child sexual abuse victims–United States—
Psychology.   2.   Incest victims–United States—
Psychology.   3.   Boys–United States–Abuse of
–Psychological aspects.   4.   Men–United States—
Psychology.   I. Title.
HQ72.U53T47   1990
362.7'6–dc20   89-13881
                                                  CIP

Launch Press
P.O.Box 31493
Walnut Creek, CA 94598
(415) 943-7603

This book is dedicated to those of us
who are survivors of incest and to the
many who still suffer from victimization.

CONTENTS

PREFACE

My name is "T" and I am a 34 year-old survivor of incest. For years I have suffered from the burdens of secrecy surrounding incest. Most of my life has been spent keeping this secret from myself. Secrecy is what makes being an incest survivor such a devastating experience for many survivors. Our abusers molested us and then made us believe it was our fault. Or perhaps we tried to tell a parent about what had happened to us and were given anger, disbelief, and threats. Soon we learned to distrust our perceptions of reality, and this has plagued many of us throughout our lives.

I felt drawn to write this book as part of my recovery process, both in terms of breaking the secret which never should have been kept, and in reaching out to others who suffer physically, mentally, emotionally, and spiritually under the burden of their incestuous secret. Many courageous women have paved the way of hope in recovery from the devastation of incest by their willingness to speak out on behalf of themselves and those who continue to be victimized by sexual abuse. Their efforts have helped me greatly in my recovery process. I now recognize that sexual abuse happens to boys as well as to girls, and that initiators of incest are both male and female.

Myths persist in our society that only females are victimized by incest, that the victimizer is almost always male, and that male survivors of incest become sex offenders. Contrary to this, Honey Fay Knopp of the Safer Society Program has spent over 35 years working with men who were sexually abused as boys. Dan Sexton of Childhelp USA is a male survivor, therapist and advocate who has been outspoken on this issue for years. Mike Lew published <u>Victims No Longer</u> in 1988, the first book devoted to the recovery process for men who were sexually abused as children, adolescents, or vulnerable adults. Hank Estrada is a survivor who founded an organization called P.L.E.A., for male survivors of childhood sexual, physical, emotional abuse and neglect. Gayle

Woodsum, the Executive Director of <u>Looking Up</u>, organized the first-ever Conference for non-offending male survivors of childhood sexual abuse in February 1988, as more and more of us men began turning to Looking Up for help. (For more information on these Resources see the listing at the end of this book.) These are all empowered advocates who are not afraid to speak the truth about sexual abuse–that at least one in every three women <u>and</u> men are adult survivors of childhood sexual abuse perpetrated by men, women, and children in positions of power or authority in relation to the victim. I have met many men and women at 12-Step meetings for survivors (see Resources) whose abusers were female. And yet denial and stereotyping persist among professionals. Why do these powerful survivor advocates I have mentioned, receive so much anger from their colleagues?

Actually, a survivor of childhood sexual abuse of either sex is more likely to become a rescuer, protector or healer, than a sex offender. That means there is a higher rate of survivors in the helping professions than in the general population–<u>more</u> than one in three psychologists, social workers, clergy, therapists, law enforcement personnel, etc., are survivors of abuse. And the truth is it can be very frightening for those of us with professional status to have to face the question: "What if it happened to me?" It is sad to say that professionals in human services, law, and church often have done more to preserve denial and stereotyping around this issue than to face the truth. What has this meant in our culture for males who have been sexually victimized?

The male victim, finally having the courage to speak out on behalf of himself as an adult, is often disbelieved. The prejudice of society is now the abusive parent who says, "This is all fantasy. Besides, if something did happen to you, what are you complaining about? You are male; you are powerful...you must have initiated it!" The truth is however, that every child or dependent adult involved in the betrayal of trust called incest is innocent.

We are not big and strong as children. For those of us who were older, our physical muscles were no match for the psychological coercion or authority of an adult. The adult we felt compelled to trust betrayed us. If it were a man who violated us, we might have felt it was because we were gay and attracted him–even though we had not yet sorted out our sexual preferences in our own minds. If the abuser were a woman and we shared our confusion with another, we might have been told how lucky we were to have such loving attention from mother, aunt, or grandma. Some of us identified with feminist feelings of being oppressed, since we grew up in a patriarchy or matriarchy. Then we felt ashamed of being male, part of the "oppressive patriarchy." Did we secretly invite the abuse? We were too confused and not yet strong enough to respond with a resounding "NO!" So we kept silent. We longed for love, understanding, and respect, and received emotional and sexual manipulation. "Sex is what all men want anyway." We did not want sex. And we were still boys whose "NO" would not be heard or respected. Sexual abuse does not respect gender. But society's professionals said it did not happen to boys. We felt isolated, not knowing there were millions more like us, all alone, all over this country.

I believe it is time for male survivors to share in print that we too have been innocent victims of childhood sexual abuse, and that with love and acceptance we can also survive and thrive. The dynamics and feelings of men and women who were sexually abused as children do not seem to be significantly different from each other. We both know fear, humiliation, betrayal, rage, anxiety, numbness, self-doubt, and confusion. We often hate ourselves because of the very sex we are. We fear close relationships with those of the sex of our abuser. Some of us fear closeness to anyone. I consider opposite sex fear another blow dealt us by our abusers which serves to isolate us even more from those who might help in the healing process.

This book is written for men who have been victimized by trusted persons and who have continued to victimize ourselves through self-destructive behavior. This book is intended for men and boys who like me, have been told that incest could not possibly have happened. It did. And we were innocent victims who are now struggling to grow into healed survivors. I believe that if we are ever to heal, each of us must begin to share his story in a place of acceptance and safety. I have found safe places among trusted friends, with fellow male survivors, and with men and women survivors in an anonymous fellowship. Incest Survivors Anonymous (ISA) and Survivors of Incest Anonymous (SIA) are fellowships comprised of victims and survivors of incest and other forms of sexual abuse. Members share their experience, strength, and hope with one another so that they may recover from the devastation of incest and help others who still suffer. These programs are based on "12-Step" recovery originally developed by Alcoholics Anonymous. The opinions I express in this book are strictly my own and are not intended as representative of any of these fellowships. I am not anonymous within my fellowship of sharing, nor do I keep secret here in print what I was forbidden to speak of within my family. I do, however, disguise my name in this book since anonymity at the level of the press is considered to be a spiritual foundation of the 12-Step Anonymous program tradition.

Mutual support is essential in the healing process and has been my motivating force in speaking out. I hope that you too will begin to feel such support as you read my sharing and begin to develop your own network of support. With heartfelt gratitude I thank those dear friends of mine who have loved me over the years until I have begun to be able to love myself. You are my non-survivor friends who believed in me and my story when I was so ready to discredit my feelings and experiences. You are also fellow survivors who understand in a way no one else can what it was like to be violated and how I still feel years afterwards. You are the advocates of those who continue to be victimized by incest and its long-term effects. By ourselves and together, we are learning that we are beautiful, unique, and lovable persons who need be victimized no more.

In Healing and Hope,

T. Thomas

ACKNOWLEDGMENTS

Men surviving childhood sexual abuse by male and female per-petrators is a topic which continues to challenge and sometimes frighten certain segments of both the therapeutic and survivor communities. It is a highly political issue both for those who insist that incest rarely happens to anyone as well as for those who con-tend it is purely a male perpetrator-female victim issue. Yet for most of us who have been victimized by sexual violence, it is a deeply personal issue transcending sexual stereotypes and de-manding a lifegiving restructuring of the social order.

When I began working on this book in the early part of 1988, there was nothing in print for non-offending male survivors, never mind written by us. Following an eight-month search of sur-vivor-friendly publishers and advocates, I had the good fortune to become associated with John Lynch and Eliana Gil of Launch Press. I am grateful to them for the groundbreaking work they have done on the various issues associated with childhood abuse and adult survivors. I am especially appreciative of their willing-ness to extend such advocacy in a specific way to male survivors of childhood sexual abuse and their support for me in this project. A special "thank you" to Fay Honey Knopp, Hank Estrada, and Dan Sexton who read my manuscript in its early form and strongly encouraged me to knock on every door until I found the right publisher. And I am glad I did.

INTRODUCTION

Am I an Incest Survivor?

This can be a puzzling question for those who do not have incest memories yet feel "something happened" as children that makes us feel uncomfortable now as adults. Below are some questions we can ask ourself. There is no "passing grade" that means we were sexually violated as children. But any yes answers can help us say: "Maybe I need to look into this more by reading literature on sexual abuse, talking with a trusted therapist or someone at a Rape Crisis Center, or attending some meetings of Survivors of Incest Anonymous or Incest Survivors Anonymous."

-Do I get very emotional when I hear incest being talked about, or else not seem to be moved at all?

-Do I sometimes wonder, "Could I have been sexually abused?" Or else strongly insist, "That never could have happened to me!"

-Do I consider my parents to have been either "Ideal parents" or "Abusive parents?"

-Do I sometimes "spaceout" or otherwise lose touch with my body?

-Do I suffer from high blood pressure, migraine headaches, back pain, chronic indigestion, throat problems, genital problems, queasy stomach, or overly-tensed muscles?

-Are there gaps in my childhood memories--even if I can remember certain early memories?

-Did anyone in my family abuse alcohol, tranquilizers, food, or other drugs?

-Am I secretive around the way I eat or drink?

-Am I always working or always doing for others?

-Do I have sleeping difficulties or troubling dreams?

-Do I get very depressed and sometimes fantasize about suicide?

-Have I ever attempted suicide or tried to hurt myself in any way?

-When people show me affection, do I feel they will also want sex?

-Does criticism feel like abuse or rejection to me?

-Does change cause me to become very anxious?

-Am I afraid of the dark?

-Do I feel uncomfortable around someone who happens to be a certain sex or wear a particular cologne?

-Can anxiety or panic sometimes flood me for no apparent reason?

-Do I go in for the "layered look" when I dress, or else feel I am always supposed to look attractive?

-Am I preoccupied with having sex or else wish relationships did not have to have a sexual component?

-Does anger--my own or others'--scare me?

-Do I believe that if people really knew me they would reject me?

-Do I either rarely cry or cry often without really knowing why?

-Do I feel different from other people?

-Am I secretly ashamed of who I am, fearing I am really bad and unworthy of love?

-Do I feel like I put on a false front to others, that I am a fake?

-Do I find it difficult to feel my feelings?

-Do I feel like a failure no matter what I do or accomplish?

-Do the people I am drawn to in relationship end up putting me down, betraying my trust, or abusing me in some way?

-Do I work in one of the helping professions or secretly feel I would be good at that sort of work?

I.

The Devastation of Incest

I grew up and lived in an abusive home for 17½ years, but I've carried those abusive attitudes toward myself for most of my life. I believed I came from a good and loving home with wonderful parents who always had my best interests at heart. They told me this in words and in some genuinely caring parenting. But the actions which conflicted with their stated ideals, the incest, they denied. My parents considered home and religion to be the most important parts of life. Dad worked for the government and in a variety of second jobs as far back as I can remember. Ma was the self-sacrificing homemaker who managed the family budget with nary an indulgence for herself. There were three children in our family including my older sister Jean and my younger sister Sara. Praying together with my parents and sisters and actively participating in church were important parts of life, and it seemed to me we did it more than other families. We did a lot together. Ma always said we children ought to play among ourselves because her parents taught her not to go outside the family. She had no adult friends who were not relatives. Dad almost always missed birthdays and celebrations because he started "celebrating" with alcohol. He had lots of friends he never spent time with otherwise. Everyone in town seemed to know Dad and vice-versa. I felt I owed a great deal to my parents because of how much they loved me even though I had bad eyesight and was too shy and not good at doing anything but school work. I never had a sense of being lovable or valuable as a person. Instead, I tried to please my parents and head off the crises precipitated by my mother's frazzled nerves or my dad's drinking. I was not very successful.

When I was 30 and shared with Ma some of my struggles to feel loved in my life, she teared up and said, "I'm sorry you feel that way T, but your father and I always loved you." My parents, two sisters and I, suffered a long time from the denial that persisted in our family. Indeed there was something terribly wrong, and the secret of incestuous abuse was the worst part.

I wasn't quite 22 when, my perfect family still intact, I fell apart. No one called it a depression, though that is what I learned it was years later in therapy. Its effects lasted a year and a half. I slept a lot, had unexpected angry outbursts, saw double (when I could focus at all), had lots of nightmares, had to use all my concentration just to hold a glass of juice or climb a flight of stairs, would drop things or have my legs fall out from under me when walking, and feared I was going crazy. Two hospitalizations for batteries of neurological tests showed no secretly hoped for brain tumor to relieve me of life. My diagnosis was "overwork and hypoglycemia." When things did not get better with time or diet, my internist said, "Sometimes the internal head pressure you are feeling is brought on by subconscious anxiety. Is there anything that has been bothering you? "Other than my physiological symptoms, I'm fine," I responded. And I genuinely meant it. Several months later I went for a psychological evaluation and began therapy.

The first year in therapy I worked on a lot of resentment towards my father. I felt he had let me down growing up. His alcoholism was a big issue for which I blamed myself. When I finally confronted him I was surprised at how openly he responded. When I was 26, he died of cancer and I felt as though we had become friends. I also felt, "Thank God it wasn't Ma who died. How would I ever survive without her?" As of yet I had no memories of incest.

During my late twenties, I began to feel that my mother wasn't the perfect person she always taught me she was, and that I had so needed to believe. I began to realize my self-hatred had its roots in my upbringing, where Ma taught me that because I was a male I was less of a person. Being quiet, good, the family peacemaker, and an "A" student couldn't erase the fact that I had a penis. In our matriarchy she had asked me to share a bedroom with Dad (twin beds) from the ages of 3 to 15. She didn't want any more children, always rebuffed Dad's signs of affection toward her in front of us children, and didn't want to deal with him coming in late at night–drunk.

Images came to me in therapy about how I used to fantasize being a girl to please my mother or being rescued by the "Lost in Space" TV family to be carried off far away. I felt humiliated when my mother dressed me in my older sister's hand-me-down clothes at age 5. She shut me up and forbade any protest. I always tried to smile, afraid of being slapped for showing my tears and my anger. Ma had a very explosive anger. Mostly she yelled, and when she did, it confirmed what I already felt–what a horrible, little, unwanted monster I really was. Why did I have to be born a disgusting boy!? It should be no surprise that I used to have dreams and daydreams of being shown love and care by a woman only after I had eaten her feces and drunk her urine. Wasn't that what I deserved? I was so confused.

While these memories and feelings resurfaced, I used to long for clear memories of my mother's abuse or love of me. But she had always given me double signals and then denied the abusive side of them. No wonder I felt crazy! My one flashback to sexual abuse came at a retreat by the ocean when I was 27. A male friend pulled a prank in my room. When I returned and discovered it I flew into a rage and wanted to kill him. (Now I look back and can say, "Thank God, I finally allowed myself to feel!"). He had invaded my boundaries and touched my clothes. I verbally expressed my anger to him and went to cool off by the ocean. This invasion of my privacy by him, opened me to a sickening feeling in my stomach. Out of nowhere an inner voice told me Uncle Willie had molested me when I was 5. I could not push it out of my mind, yet I had no clear memories of <u>how</u> he had violated me. Later, when I shared this with a counselor, I was assured it was symbolic of something other than actual sexual abuse. I accepted his interpretation, but deep down I could no longer wall off the awareness that there were sexual aspects to my childhood abuse.

As I turned 30 I began to have dreams that I did not comprehend for two or three years. As a child I had often dreamt of my home being invaded, of my being all alone against an enemy army, and of being powerless and paralyzed as I was attacked. But in time those fears of invasion turned into a numb resignation. Two adult recollections illustrate....

I dreamt of waking up inside a young woman's vagina which was giant-sized. Bob, her brother, was also inside. I was terrified, angry, hurt, and frustrated because I had trusted her as a friend. Now I was overwhelmed by this giant woman. Bob was casual and matter of fact when he said, "Don't worry about it. This is where they (women) keep us. There is nothing we can do about it anyway." A few years later I had another terrifying flashback. I am a crying infant. My mother stifles my cries by pressing me tightly against her breasts and I cannot breathe. I am suffocating.... Now she presses me against her crotch. The smell is overpowering... the darkness, the moistness, the feeling of a warm monster, alive and wanting to devour me whole.... No wonder I became numb.

I dream another time... A friend of mine, Elaine, takes me under a car lift in a garage. There is a man's body lying on it above us, It is her husband. His testicles drop down, and hang loose. Very casually, as if she were talking to me while kneading dough, Elaine demonstrates how I ought to "service" a man every so often. It is not so difficult, she assures me. I am repulsed by the sight, smell, touch, and atmosphere of the whole scene which I cannot erase from my memory. I remember that Elaine was molested as a girl and sexually abused by her husband in marriage. A few years later I realized the dream referred to Uncle Willie exposing himself to me when I was 5 and pushing my face into his genitals. I can no longer respond matter of factly to this anguish. The thought of oral sex makes me want to vomit and wish I could pass out.

"You cheap prick, son of a bitch!" The litany would begin late at night. In the kitchen. Through the bedroom wall against which I slept. I froze in my bed, startled out of protective sleep by the screeching, knife-like bursts of Ma's voice directed at Dad upon his late-night arrival from the bar. I know I was very young because Ma had not yet given up yelling at Dad when he came in drunk. "That's not a daytime swear Ma uses at Dad," I thought to myself-not knowing which was worse, the screaming fight in the kitchen or its ending, meaning Dad would come into "our" room. "Son of a bitch is part of the daytime litany when Ma is mad and yells at him. But what is this 'cheap prick?' It must be something awful because she only uses it at night when he's drunk–before he rips the phone out of the wall, breaks dishes, or kicks a door in. I want to remember it and find out what it means someday. Cheap prick, cheap prick...." I silently repeated this phrase hoping to distract my mind from the terror I felt.

When Dad came into our bedroom after he had been out drinking he staggered and stank. Sometimes he laughed that drunken laugh to himself or muttered in anger. He would try to undress and get all tangled up in his clothes. "Please God, don't let him come over to me. Stay calm. Look relaxed and asleep. Hold the covers tight, but let the comforter on top hang loose so he doesn't see me hanging on." Almost always he threw up. He tried to aim for the waste basket. I was always awake. Everyone was awake but we all pretended to sleep. Years later Ma would say, "I used to ask you if you minded sleeping with your father. I'm glad you'd say it was OK because I didn't want to sleep with him like that.." I was scared to death–but death would have been merciful.

Only in my thirties did I remember the night I left my body. Dad came in as usual. I was scared and pretended to sleep. He came over to joke and play with me. I used to feel bad that Ma would never let Dad touch her, but now I didn't want him touching me either. I had no choice. The first time I remembered, I told it matter of factly, as though I were an unemotional observer. I was an observer. When Dad touched me and scared me I did the only thing I could. I tensed up completely in my body and let my awareness float up to the ceiling in the corner of the room. I didn't even try to re-enter for another 25 years. Dad stopped playing and pulled down my pajama bottoms. He kept quietly laughing as though we were having fun. His hands were on my body... His penis rubbed up against me between my legs from behind. It was huge. I was only 3. It hurt. I HURT!!! But I kept silent. I left my body which was no longer safe and watched from above.

The next day I tried to tell Ma. She grabbed me around the neck and shoulders and exploded. "I'll kill you! I'll kill you! I'll kill you!" she screamed at the top of her lungs. I couldn't breathe. She was choking me. I was sure I had done something terribly wrong and she would cut off my penis. Two years later when my uncle molested me, I said nothing. I never spoke about incest again before leaving at 17. When I first disclosed my being violated, within the safety of a 12 Step group (Overeaters Anonymous), I choked and choked and choked. But I was determined and did not stop until I had shared the words of feeling betrayed as a child. This time I was met with acceptance by the group, by my Higher Power, and by myself.

"You must have suffered a physical trauma between your legs, behind your scrotum. The damage to your urethra was extensive and you had gone into retention. We had to do an emergency suprapubic bypass for now." The voice belonged to Dr. Weinstein, my urologist. It was 20 years after the attack. I had never known a "normal" urination or ejaculation. It always hurt. "No, doctor, no one in my family has had urologic problems that I know of. No, I don't remember any objects hurting me between my legs. When I was younger? Well, I don't remember. My testicles sometimes hurt a lot–they have since puberty–but my physician had said nothing was physically abnormal. Maybe it was just strain. I've never been able to masturbate. And when I've had an ejaculation in my sleep lately, I've almost gone through the roof in pain. I had come to you because of this and because my urine flow was now literally reduced to drop-by-drop." He responded, "Well, we will have to reconstruct your urethra once you have had time to heal. The scar tissue probably built up over a long period of time blocking it off so completely I couldn't get the tiniest catheter through." My parents had driven 200 miles each way to visit me. They must love me. I didn't even pause to reflect why I had brought Matthew and Dennis Linn's book, Healing Life's Hurts. The doctor continued, "It could have been something that happened years ago, like falling on a sharp rock." Or maybe a "cheap prick..."

In gratitude for the "parental love" I felt I did not deserve as a child, I always stayed at home and tried to be a good boy for my mother. She never had any adult friends besides one of her sisters and seemed very unhappy and stressed. "Your mother's a saint," Dad would say. Years later he added, "It was her prayers that helped me stop drinking." Dad always took the family out on Sundays. We'd go for rides or to the beach or mountains and have good times. But it is the Saturday outings I remember all too painfully. From when I was about 7 until I left at 17, he and I would usually work together around the house for awhile. Then he'd wink and say, "C'mon T, let's go for a respite." We'd go to a bar. He'd buy me chips and a Coke. He talked with his friends and drank beers beyond number. Sometimes he finished beers left by other patrons. Hours later, usually after several subdued pleadings, he would agree to come home. That is why I was there–to see him home. It was an unwritten agreement among Ma, Dad, and me. It happened even on my graduation day. I was Valedictorian. We made it on time because I called my sister who drove down and together we outvoted him. I always felt responsible for getting him home and always a failure because he always got there drunk. It was horrible to be with him when he drank and worse not to know where he was or if he'd get killed while all alone. Ma said Dad was too scrupulous to ever fool around with another woman–but apparently not with his own son. Maybe I didn't take care of him well enough.

I did my best. At age 3, I went with him to see a "bad man" who lived out in the country, in the woods, up a hill, on an isolated drive. "He might have a gun," Dad said nervously. And I knew he was mad at Dad. I clung tightly to his hand. I was Dad's protector. We survived.

It was just this year I confronted my abusers with my feelings. Uncle Willie and Dad in the cemetery along with both sets of grandparents for the unhealthy parenting passed on. Jean and Sara and Ma felt devastated by the letter and reprints of my sharings from survivor journals that I sent my mother. And they claimed deep concern for me. "You must have been under a lot of pressure to concoct such gruesome lies about our parents," Sara angrily responded. "Someone must have really messed up your head," she added. When we talked in person, Sara (who shared a bed with my mother through childhood) gave me all the reasons why nothing could have happened to me. Ma said she wanted to respect my feelings. Unknown to me, she had called two persons with whom I live to see if I was "alright." She told them she was afraid I might harm myself or her. She also assured me that she did not do the things I remember, although she felt she really could not handle being a mother. The following week she wrote me a letter saying, "How can I say a million times I am sorry for not being a better mother to you..." Communication has been difficult for me with her. I never wanted a <u>better</u> or <u>best</u> mother. I only wanted to be loved and respected for the person I was and the person I am. I also did not want my personal boundaries violated. This my parents were unable to give me. Today I am a good mother and father to myself. I trust in a loving God very different from the God-of-my-misunderstanding, that I grew up with. And I seek out healthy and healing relationships that nurture me and challenge me to grow.

No question about it–the heritage of incest I received has been devastating. I write in order to share the good news that there is recovery and hope. In many ways my parents genuinely tried to love me. But that does not erase the violence of incest, nor absolve them of their responsibility. In accepting responsibility for my own life, I began a process of healing and I began a new life. I still feel love for the members of my family of origin along with distrust and betrayal. Today I recognize my right to say "NO!" to unhealthy relationships with them. I am an incest survivor on my life journey from victimization to surviving to thriving. In the following pages I share with you some aspects in my process of recovery. I hope it serves as a source of encouragement for you as you seek to recover from the devastation of incest.

II.

A Journal of Recovery

I have chosen twelve different recovery issues to discuss. Each area can contribute to keeping the secret of our abusive past from ourselves as well as preventing lifegiving changes in our lives. Each area can be met with courage, honesty, and openness and become a key to healing, freedom from victimization, and a new life as a survivor. This is not an exhaustive list by any means. I have found these issues to be critical for me and other survivors. I have chosen to write about them in journal form based on my experiences. Perhaps you will want to begin your own journal of recovery in response to each of these concerns or to add your own.

1. Trust

I have been afraid of persons, places, and things for most of my life. I have had a difficult time trusting anyone because I could never really trust myself. On the outside I was serious, attentive to others, and perceived as trustworthy. When others viewed me in these ways I felt counterfeit because they didn't know how I really was. If they ever did, I feared they would certainly reject me.

Many survivors of incest become helping professionals or at least focus more on others than themselves. This was true for me. I entered the ministry. In the midst of my severe depression I graduated from college and was sent to teach in a high school run by the religious denomination to which I belonged. However, at that point in time the most ministry I was up to was washing dishes (alone) and working two hours a day as a library aide. I felt that no one wanted me. I couldn't do anything right. My energy level was so low. Yet during this year in the South, a man and woman came into my life who taught me a lot about love and acceptance and gave me the courage to begin to trust.

Len was the high school principal and my spiritual mentor. His actions told me he valued me as a person no matter what it I was able to do. This was entirely new to me, and initially hard to trust. "Why would he love me?" "He didn't want sex from me." "He didn't want me to take care of him." "He valued my opinions and feelings." This did not compute.

In his outgoing and caring way Len reminded me of Dad, but with a big difference. He could be just as spontaneous with anger as he could with tenderness–and neither feeling destroyed him (or me). Expressions of anger were forbidden in my childhood home for anyone but my mother (because her anger was righteous). It was OK for Len to be Len. It was OK for me to be "T." It was OK to be imperfect. When I did something wrong that didn't mean I was a bad person. Not only was it OK to be human, it was enjoyable (and scary). I really wanted for myself what I saw in Len. I felt a deep love for him as a man and a father figure. Through the acceptance and love of self he shared with me I felt as though I were beginning to learn to trust, love, and accept myself. I began to learn that men could be beautiful and free persons. Len gave me permission for the first time in my life to feel OK about loving and hating my Dad. I can't say I really developed self-love yet, but I accepted another's love. I was then able to begin to love myself.

Before moving down South I had been touched deeply by my Higher Power in two healing prayer meetings I had been invited to attend by friends. There was a prayer meeting in a church basement about a mile away from this high school but for a long time I didn't go. Instead, I drowned my fears with alcohol and sugar. One day I got fed up with stuffing my feelings and went to the prayer meeting. I felt envious of two young people who seemed to pray joyfully and spontaneously. I thought they could pray that way because they hadn't experienced hard times in life. I found out I was wrong. Soon I was taking the Life in the Spirit seminars led by the mother of one of those teens.

I had been told growing up that I was loved. But I often felt more like an unwanted burden than a lovable gift in the family. I was God's mistake. Yet among this prayer group and from my teacher Nettie, I began to learn about love that was nothing like the double messages I had known. I didn't have to humiliate myself in order to be loved. I didn't have to give over my body sexually or prostitute my emotions in order to be loved. I was loved without doing, performing, and without a demand for payoff. It was wonderful and it was terrifying. This couldn't be right. I must be fooling them. How come they couldn't see how bad I really was?

I was not yet ready or able to see that it had been my parents and uncle who had done bad things. I was not aware that I was still protecting and defending them. But Nettie and the others just continued to love me and accept me without judgement or intrusion. Ten years later when I tearfully shared with Nettie that I was an incest survivor, she responded that she had often thought I had been an abused child. Today I know that Nettie was confronting me with nurturing love, not by taking my inventory or reading the history behind my fears. By her actions she taught me that healthy mothers love differently than mine did.

This was the first grade of the school where I began to learn trust. There have been many more lessons and teachers since. But this is where I began to believe that trust grows out of the freedom to enter into caring, unpretentious relationships which are rooted in love and acceptance.

2. Addictions

Dad drank. Ma overate. I did both. Overeating originally started for me at about age 7. If only I gained weight and wasn't so scrawny maybe my parents would love me. So I gained lots of weight. At home food was a sign of affection that was permitted. My childhood fantasy was of the living room full of M & M's. Yet I knew that even if I were able to eat them all I would'n feel better. I would be too numb and sick to feel anything. but in a certain sense, that was better.

With Dad's alcoholism and Ma's anger over it, drinking while I still lived at home was not an option. I started drinking gradually when I was 18. "Gradually" meant drinking as much as possible without throwing up. The frequency increased through my twenties as I found the magic relief which alcohol provided.

By the time I was 28 it just wasn't working anymore. I ate mounds of food, drank more and more, worked constantly, and kept my mind occupied by memorizing all kinds of professional sports statistics as an armchair athlete. Despite all this, I could no longer constrict my feelings. Eating and drinking made me feel sick to my stomach. Meanwhile, my blood pressure skyrocketed so high I was afraid of having a stroke. And I couldn't stop my addictions.

Through Alcoholics Anonymous and Overeaters Anonymous I began to find a hope for recovery in my life. I realized I wasn't alone anymore. I found out there were lots of other lonely, confused, scared people like me, and that through these programs many had found recovery, life, and a genuine sense of happiness. Their problems didn't disappear–but they weren't as terrified any more.

Today I don't eat or drink substances which have caffeine, processed sugar, bleached flour, or alcohol. I feel better and my mind is more clear. Sometimes I get the urge to drink or overeat. Just for today I know I do not have to give in to these urges. If I take the time to listen to my feelings I realize that usually I am hungry or thirsty for something much more basic–like human concern, understanding, warmth and acceptance.

There are many others like me who have come to accept the reality of our incestuous abuse through the recovery programs of Alcoholics Anonymous, Overeaters Anonymous, Narcotics Anonymous, AlAnon/Adult Children, and others. For those of us who may be more prone to getting hooked on addicting, self-abusing substances, these programs have helped to clear our minds and our feelings. This clarity allows us to begin to feel what we have so deeply repressed.

I want to state clearly, that not all incest survivors go on to become addicted to a particular substance. That is no more true than saying that incest survivors become sex offenders. I believe the truth is that those of us who were victimized incestuously learned at the hands of a once-trusted person what it is to be victimized. Some of us who were biochemically prone to substance addiction have become so addicted thus perpetuating the victimization once perpetrated against us. Some of us have become victimized in other relationships in our lives because we never learned healthy ways of relating. All of us have something deeper and stronger within us that enables us (howsoever painfully) to survive our victimization. It is this inner life-force, human-value, or God-image upon which our recovery is built.

3. Physical Problems

Sometimes there is direct physical damage as a result of incest. This may be due to the size and strength difference between a larger, stronger attacker who exerts force and a small victim with a fragile, forming body. Physical damage can occur from anal, genital, or oral abuse. Broken bones and sexually transmitted diseases, including AIDS and venereal disease are also consequences of sexual abuse. While this type of physical harm may seem more obvious, I have already stated that I made no connection for many years between my genito-urinary damage and an awareness of sexual violence done to me as a very young child.

Other physiological damage is not so obvious or easy to link with sexual abuse. However, we are physiological, psychological, spiritual entities, and the traumatic stress of abuse when held inside for years wears on our bodies as well as our spirits.

From physiological studies of the cardiovascular system, Dr. James Lynch (1985) has linked hypertension and migraine headaches to a learned attitude of hypervigilance towards a world perceived as threatening. He does not make the connection to incest, per se, but I can certainly see where it would apply. He does go on to state, however, that these diseases are symptomatic in persons who have become disconnected from their bodies. From a spiritual perspective, Louise Hay (1982) asserts that visual problems are related to a child's not wanting to see things which are transpiring in the home. She further relates the disease of glaucoma to pressure from longstanding hurts. I have this disease with no family history of it–though it is generally thought to be congenital and to develop after the age of 40. The hypervigilant stance I developed early in life has also affected me physically in terms of having overly tensed, aching muscles.

One could go to the extreme of relating every ache and pain to incest. This is not my intention. Rather, our bodies were affected by incest beyond the duration of the acts. In order to deal with this I have sought different types of bodywork with gentle and caring practitioners of both sexes and I have been able to release the feelings so tightly locked within.

Physical healing for me has meant moving away from an attitude of self-blame and resentment of others. These feelings prevent my forming relationships and isolate me from the love and care I long for in order to thrive. I have come to see that I am my body and that I am OK. I am growing to love my body as I am and to accept my eyes and urinary tract and blood vessels in my imperfections. These aspects of my physical self have been through hell and have survived. What a wonderful accomplishment! I am valuable and lovable in all my body and in all my person. I have my wounds, but I am also healing.

4. Sexuality

We incest survivors have sexualities as varied and as splendid as anyone else. We have in common the fact that our sexuality was cruelly violated at a vulnerable stage of our development. We are wounded in this area. It is unwise to make universal statements about the sexuality of survivors. Like everyone else, we are unique and varied sexual beings.

Some of us have grown into adulthood fairly comfortable with our sexuality, meeting and choosing loving partners. Many others of us have not been fortunate enough to feel comfortable in the world either singly or with a partner. For us, sexuality has represented the shame and guilt of our victimization.

I always feared personal closeness and warmth from others, whether male or female, because I thought a sexual payoff would be demanded. Survivors who have shared this fear cope in different ways. Some became promiscuous, longing for love but feeling betrayed, victimized and isolated afterwards. Others abstain from sexual intimacy completely. I chose a lifestyle where sexual abstinence was considered a virtue. In reality, it was needed protection from further violation. While I have met survivors for whom compulsive masturbation to the point of bleeding became a problem, I have never been able to masturbate to ejaculation.

It is untrue to say that those who have been sexually abused are sexually aware. In fact, the opposite can happen. The only awareness I had of sexuality is that it was something frightful and forbidden. I blocked out everything else having to do with sex. My parents were excessively modest in dress and my mother learned from her parents that husband and wife should express no affection towards each other in front of the children. Instead, I would see her freeze up, clench her teeth, and shove my father away whenever he wanted to give her a hug or a peck on the cheek. It made what happened to me all the more a living nightmare which I could not remember.

Somehow I felt being fat protected me both from sexual attention and from closeness. If others stayed away from me, I wouldn't have to deal with my sexual feelings. Because my father sexually abused me I felt different from other boys. I also assumed I was gay. Attitudes around me encouraged my shame and secrecy. I had my first close friendship with another young man after I left home at 17. We were never sexually intimate although I was quite fond of him and found him attractive. At 22, I felt warmth and closeness with another man my age. We got into necking and were in bed at one point. I felt it was OK since I really wasn't in my body. But when he started "coming" on top of me and stroking my penis, I got very scared and left. Sometimes when friendships with men develop I can become frightened that sex will be expected of me. I can feel very small and inadequate. Today I understand that sex is associated with the time when trusted adults demanded more than I as a little boy should ever have been asked.

We men who were molested as boys often believe that we are gay. There is no scientific evidence of a direct cause and effect, although the early sexual contact tends both to confuse us about our sexuality and allow negative projections to potential lovers who are the same sex as our offender. But an offender cannot make a person gay, straight, or bisexual. We are what we are. In my healing sexuality I feel attracted to women and men, though predominantly women. Our true sexual preferences come from inside ourselves; they cannot be imposed on us by our offenders.

I never wanted to act on sexual feelings towards men or women; I did not want to be like the abusers. I was embarassed and ashamed at having an erection with a man or woman I liked. It felt like another betrayal. I also felt "less than a man," because I spurned sex. It was not until I was 28 that I "went all the way" with a woman fifteen years my elder. She was loving and kind, yet the experience was devastating for me. It literally took years to work out my feelings around that intimacy–and I was fortunate to find that Hannah was more interested in me than in having sex–and that we did not have to relate that way any more in order to be friends. It is scary living in a world where every time a man or woman moves close, abuse seems the only possibe outcome. Two other relationships with women my own age helped to break the lie of all-pervasive abuse that had begun to crack with Hannah.

I met Katherine through a common interest in the healing arts. We shared a history of deeply wounded childhoods. Our inner responses to abuse had been to open to our healing capacities. With each other we learned that healing love could be received as well as given, that tenderness and affection did not demand sexual payoffs, nor was a mutual choice for non-genital expressions of love "less."

Lynn, on the other hand, was the one person I ever seriously considered as a life partner–and she, me. I have never known sexual love elsewhere to be so passionate and gently trusting, so enjoyable and mutually healing in physical, emotional and spiritual ways.

Today I choose to live in a healing community of men and women. I choose to do so while being celibate. It feels right for me. All my formative years men and women had access to my bed and to my body. I feel so good just to be able to sleep alone and safe. I also choose to meet my deep need for interpersonal intimacy through celibate loving. That works for me. Others find that having a partner feels right for them. What is important to me as we move from victim to survivor and from isolation to community is the realization that today we have a choice of how we want to live as sexual beings. There is no "right way"–only a way that is right for each of us.

5. Destructive Relationships

Some time ago my acupuncturist recommended I read <u>Women Who Love Too Much</u> (Norwood, 1986) and change the pronouns from "she" to "he." She was right. I saw myself on most pages of that book. Men and women survivors learned the victim role through incest. Some of us do grow up to live out the perpetrator role, yet most of us continue as victims hoping someone will truly love us. Secretly we fear rejection if others get too close.

I have always been attracted to women like the mother of my childhood, who give double messages. For many years I unconsciously attempted to win my mother's love by gaining love and acceptance from similar women I met. It was as though I had special radar seeking these women out. But because they too were sick, all they could offer me was abuse. It hurt, but it was a familiar pain. I really didn't know there was anything else. These women would act affectionately towards me at times and subsequently conveyed the message that I, like all men, was worthless. I believed them because I believed the message myself. In that way I was very much my mother and father's son.

These relationships affected me in similar ways to alcohol and sugar. The booze and the M & M's never filled the inner void or healed my ache. These relationships each promised to do so–at least temporarily. As harmful as they were for me, equally powerful was my attraction to them. I learned to apply the same principles to these relationships as I do to food and alcohol: Don't take the first bite, drink, phone call. The insane thought that "This time her kind words won't end up in a put down" is akin to the thought, "This time just one drink/bite won't end up in a binge."

Just as there is healthy food and drink that nourish the body, so are there healthy relationships that nourish the spirit. I believe more and more that I deserve to have friends of both sexes who care for me without turning on me and hitting me over the head. I am delighted to have friends with whom there is a true mutuality, not a one up or one down dynamic. It is so much healthier to be able to love such friends and feel good about myself as a result of the friendship. Someone once said that in friendship we receive the gift of ourselves. This is so true when we leave the victim role behind and become survivors.

6. Amnesia

A person awakens from a blow to the head only to see a strange and unfamiliar world. Memory provides no information about the identity of persons gathered around. To the concerned questions, "Who are you?" and "What happened to you?" the confused person draws a blank. How fearful to be in the middle of life and have no bearings and no sense of self!

We have all seen versions of this scenario in books, television, and the movies. Many of us who survived childhood incest or other abuse have lived our lives in just this way. Oh yes, we recognize who our parents and relatives are and we know our own names. But we often have a very confused sense of self, anxiety about our lives, and an inexplicable fearfulness around certain persons and situations.

I began the long road of therapy at 22, still in the midst of a debilitating depression. My friend Mark consoled me saying, "When you get through this you'll discover that there is nothing wrong with you at all." Inside there were feelings that terribly hurtful things had happened to me. Outside my parents had always said, "That's crazy. Nothing happened. We love you." So I believed my parents loved me and that I was both crazy and ungrateful in return. Mark had known there was nothing bad about me and I wanted to believe it too, but I had no memory of the personal, sexual violations I had suffered. These would not come for years.

For those of you like me who have struggled with these awful feelings of anxiety, stress, and fear with nothing that explains them, perhaps you have suffered some amnesia also. Bear in mind that I've always had an excellent memory. Throughout my adult life I have remembered some events dating back to age two. But memory gaps around specific ages can be signs of possible denial or repression. Both of these are powerful psychological forces which allow a person to endure an incredible amount of trauma. Denial is not to be confused with conscious lying. Nor is repression a wanting to forget something unpleasant. Both are involuntary and unconscious operations designed to preserve the stability of the psyche through traumatic events. Ideally, the unconscious will become conscious knowledge and memory when the person is better equipped to deal with the trauma. However, the effects are often long-lasting because incest is so personally devastating. Then, like the person in the movies who gets whacked on the head with a rock, I cannot remember try as I may. When the unnameable pain gets too intense many of us seek therapy.

I had gone through years of therapy and had concluded, "I don't have specific memories to fit the feelings of my incestuous abuse. Perhaps I never will. What is important for me is that I trust my feelings as true and get on with my life now." Eventually I remembered about Uncle Willie and a few years later about Ma and Dad. There may yet be other things I need to remember for my healing and growth. But I trust that in time my Higher Power will lead me to whatever I need to see and feel. When the feelings and memories come now, I choose to honor myself with trust and acceptance. In that sense I am at peace.

7. Troubling Dreams

My experience tells me that my dreams do not lie. In fact, in highly symbolic language they communicate to me many of the feelings and experiences that have disappeared from my conscious awareness. Sleep is a time of letting go, and I have come to believe that in that place of receptivity my loving Higher Power is the Dream Maker who speaks to me. The voice (and the message) is not always pleasant, but it is a continuing means of much growth and hope for me. Often what has long been buried through denial or repression becomes available through my dreams. I am too close to my dreams to try to comprehend them myself, so I explore their meaning with a trusted therapist. It is important to say that he does not tell me what my dreams mean but helps me discover that within myself.

Earlier I mentioned my childhood nightmares of being invaded. Some 20-25 years later this nightmare returned in slightly altered form. I was being held by KGB agents near my present home at the same time that President Reagan declared war on China. In captivity, I fell asleep for awhile. Upon awakening I was told by the agents that a heart surgeon had implanted a razor-like device inside the major artery of my heart. I was shown a small jewelry box one agent held which contained a diamond pin. He said that if he pulled the pin out, a timing device would be set in motion to activate a painful death in me. Even though I had no physical evidence of having had surgery, I was too scared to disbelieve them. Eventually the U.S. ransomed me at no real cost. The secret police let me go but held the pin that ensured my silence.

The truth is that my parents let me go at 17, but all these years they've held the diamond pin that terrified me into keeping my mouth shut. Only in recovery have I realized they cannot cut off the lifeblood to my heart. They cannot make me keep the secret of incest. Disclosing the secret didn't kill me, it gave me life.

Last Fall I had a frightening dream. I was with an 8 year-old nephew of mine at the home of a couple who played all kinds of tricks on us. I could not relate to anyone there because everything kept changing. I finally saw that this man and woman were "tricksters" and thereupon left the house. Once outside, I remembered that little Tommy was still inside. I went back and found him sitting in a darkened room. The Tommy I'd arrived with was happy, trim, and energetic; this boy was fat, docile, disheveled, and scared. Looking at him I knew he had been molested. The man and woman tricksters laughed at my allegations and called me crazy. Then they worked some magic that changed my looks too. But they could not hold us. I held Tommy lovingly close to myself as we left–changed, but free... I understand the dream to mean that only I can take responsibility for the little boy inside myself who was ravaged by his own parents. Yes, I have been changed by what happened to me as a child, but no, I don't have to be victimized by it anymore. I walked out of my parents' home a free man.

There are many more dreams which I will not share here. These two are typical of my troubling dreams that have given me hope. Dreams that re-present the feelings associated with our incest experiences can be terribly frightening and threatening. What could be worse than being violated and betrayed by a loved one? Someone we were so dependent upon? Someone we looked to for love and support? When I remember a dream, write it down, and share it with another in confidence, I have already broken the taboo of silence. I have shared feelings I was once forbidden to feel or speak–even if that sharing comes in dream symbols I don't fully understand. As I do this I take one more step in the direction of freedom and new life.

8. Feelings

I used to think that someone suffering from Post-Traumatic Stress Disorder (PTSD) had to have fought in the jungles of Southeast Asia or been imprisoned in a Nazi concentration camp. And when I herd the term, "out-of-body experience," I would think of a mystic, or a person who had been resuscitated from near-death. What a surprise to learn that both are part of my own life experience as a survivor! I never fought in Vietnam and I was never imprisoned in a concentration camp. I grew up in a place where I was told I was loved, then abused, next told it never happened, and finally threatened with death if I ever spoke out. It was an experience shared by millions of other incest victims--and each of us thought we were the only one.

Feelings. What does it mean to live with the awareness that when I was a child, those I needed to trust the most did not protect and nurture me, but violated me, betrayed my trust, and stole my innocence? Can you who are survivors bear to ask yourselves this question? You are courageous if you can. Only a few months ago I remember feeling horrified at reading the tortures one woman survivor endured as a child–until I put down the paper aghast: "Oh my God, that's my story!" Many of us first feel our feelings by empathizing with others. Five years ago I was a man who burned with pain but whose tears were frozen solid. In time I became a person who cried daily the tears of anger and sorrow over my abuse.

So many of us hold our feelings tightly bound within. "If I ever let loose I'll tear down everything in sight, I'll go berserk, I'll destroy even people I care about... If I confront my perpetrator with anger, s/he will drop dead of a heart attack or stroke... I'll go completely out of control and have nothing left." These are not uncommon feelings among survivors. When I shared my hurt and anger in letters and poetry with my therapist and in survivor journals, I felt affirmed and validated. When I externalized my anger at my mother for dressing me in my sister's clothes–by working over a 75 pound punching bag with a baseball bat, under supervision–I was supported and encouraged by other survivors as a person who has a right to express his feelings and be treated with dignity. When I confronted my mother in person with my memories of childhood incest, she did not die. Buildings did not fall down. People were not destroyed. And I began to let go of what has been eating me alive for most of my life.

I have gradually been able to re-enter my body during the past few years. I don't need out-of-body experiences as a way of life anymore as I did when a small child hovering near the ceiling during my sexual abuse. I also realize I survived something which can be more terrifying to a little child than a hostile jungle or a concentration camp could be to an adult. In my professional life I have been able to be available and compassionate to persons during some very painful and scary life crises. But nowhere have I encountered the depth of pain, of rage, and of courage that I have in survivors–perhaps because it is my own. My healthy survival of traumatic abuse means that sometimes I need to shut down my emotions at any time. It is a remnant safeguard (scar) from the days of my incest. When I feel safe I can risk feeling.

Ongoing recovery includes having the safe place of a survivors' group in which I feel accepted, understood, supported, and validated. I can choose either to share my feelings or express that sharing feelings for me is too threatening. I can be with others who are concerned about living in the present but not at the cost of forgetting about the past or putting it all behind us. Being an incest survivor is a fact I cannot change. I no longer wish to deny my past. I continue to integrate it in a healing way into who I am today. In this way I believe I am opening myself to ever deepening levels of healing and growth in my life, and conveying hope for other survivors and victims.

9. Depression and Suicidal Thoughts

Depression and suicide are closely related to my understanding of God. Maybe it's because, as another minister told me, many survivors come from a home where the perpetrators of abuse were very "religious." That's where the image of the God-of-my-misunderstanding was rooted. This false God was a Powerful Person who loved me out of obligation and saw me as a regrettable mistake. I came to see myself as a miserable person who could never be good enough to please this God. I would have considered suicide if not for the fact that I believed in an afterlife and if anything infuriated God it was suicide. I felt I was left to live without hope or escape–a life of helplessness and depression.

This God-of-my-misunderstanding is a childhood portrait of my mother closely followed as well by my father. I guess every young child sees mother and father as God. It seems to me the more unhealthy our childhood "Gods" are, the more tenaciously we cling to the images. These Gods believe in control and not at all in "live and let live." After awhile depression became second nature. Compulsive overeating, alcoholism, workaholism, and self-destructive relationships became a slow suicide.

Then one day I felt loved. Feeling loved even in the smallest way and being desperate enough to want to put down the sugar, alcohol, and hurtful friends gave me the courage to look for help in taking this first step and becoming hopeful. I found it in rooms with other people very much like me who hated themselves without cause and who had abused chemicals and relationships to avoid the unbearable fear and pain that seemed always to be on the verge of overwhelming us.

In those rooms I found wounded people like myself who did not demand that I stifle my feelings. They loved me as I was. It was their love and acceptance that challenged me to grow–not by doing more, but by opening to love and affirming my own goodness. God, was that painful! And then, wonder of wonders, I began to enjoy myself and others! I found that I am more than a frightened child who is too scared to speak and always wants to hide in a corner. I began gradually loosening my grip on the God-of-my-misunderstanding and opened to a new understanding of a loving Higher Power who didn't think I was a terrible mistake, but a precious child and lovable man. As a child I always saw fear and resentment behind surface parental smiles and words of love. Today, through 12 Step and survivor groups I am growing in love with a God who wants me to have the freedom to live my own life, to experience a measure of happiness, and to feel supported in times of disappointment. Sometimes I am able to glimpse the image of that God when I pass by a mirror–the image that used to disgust me.

I still get depressed from time to time. The holidays are especially rough for me. But I accept my feelings, see to my needs as a priority, and continue to share with friends and other survivors. The depression passes, sometimes quickly, sometimes not. Once last Fall I resisted an impulse to leap in front of a truck. Later I processed the incident with my therapist. I'd like to say it's all behind me, but it's not. These are some of the after-effects of incest for me. My recovery is a lifelong process. I no longer wish for a magical life. Everyone has wounds to deal with; mine are incest wounds. Ten years ago I longed for a suspected brain tumor or cancer to relieve me of the burden of life. Today I long to live.

10. Helping Professionals

I have always wanted to help other people. I am told I do it well. I listen, I care, and I give others the space and focus they need to tap their inner strengths and connect with a Higher Power. I am even involved in a program in which I teach others how to become more effective helping professionals. I have been helping others for a very long time, before I ever had any studies or training–when I was a little boy.

Many survivors are like me–doctors, therapists, clergy, health care workers, counselors, social workers, you-name-it-helping-others. Not all incest survivors become professional helpers, but many of us do. Some of us find that we need to leave the helping professions temporarily or permanently in order to heal and live our own lives. All of us need to learn to put ourselves and our feelings first in order to recover. We learned a long time ago to function under trauma. It's living with serenity that's scary!

I have spent my adult life trying to be a compassionate friend to people in crisis, from the very young to the elderly, afflicted with various hardships in mind, body, and spirit. I didn't have the awareness of what was wrong with me or the faintest idea of how to be healed myself. So I eased (stifled) my agony by helping others. And every so often I'd get very depressed. Giving to others can be draining. It makes you keenly aware that you have not received that which you are giving.

At age 3, I'd been my Dad's protection against the angry contractor with the gun. A few years later I was seeing him safely home from bars. I always tried to make my terribly unhappy mother happy, and soothe her uncalmable anger.

Today I do not try to help my parents in other people. I continue to listen to the hurting child within me and seek the help that I need. I am responsible for no one's life but my own. And if my recovery should ever mean I need to leave the helping profession that is what I would do.

Two years ago I took some time off from full-time involvement in helping others in order to return to school. I also sought out ways of nurturing myself. I became flooded with painful feelings yet I did not become emotionally paralyzed. When I went into a six week period of depression, I was able to accept my changed needs at this time, become less demanding on myself, and share my feelings with others. The depression passed. When I do not fill my life with the excitement of other people's problems, I have room for myself and my feelings. Instead of the vague feeling of being tired and having an overstressed body, mind, and spirit I can identify feelings of joy, sadness, fear, love, anger and warmth.

Two dangers I have encountered as a helping professional and incest survivor are denial and rescuing. When I deny my incest I cannot accept others who come to me with an incestuous background. Too many of us have been hurt by therapists, pastors, and doctors who have said, "No, it couldn't have happened to you." Then there is rescuing–a futile attempt to heal myself vicariously in another. It just does not work. I have to face my own childhood sufferings and losses with all their implications for my life. I cannot do it through another's growth process. Nor can I rescue my abusers in others. Trying to save my parents in others who have reminded me of them has led me to self-destructive relationships. The truth is: I cannot help myself by being a helping professional. I can be of true service to others only if I first have the courage to face myself and my history honestly. Only then can I share the gift of recovery I have received.

11. Family of Origin

Extremes. For many years I thought my family of origin was perfect, except for me who was a terrible disappointment. I invested a lot of energy in that illusion only later to feel rage and deep hurt when it was shown to be false. Today I recognize that I grew up in a very wounded and unhealthy family system. Denial perpetuates the destruction. Awareness is the painful beginning of healing.

Emotional separation from the destructive family system from which we came is often a major issue for survivors. Yet to do so has felt like exposing my victimization to the world. Society often views survivors as irreparably damaged. Male survivors are often assumed to be future abusers. I would like to share one story to show how far from the truth this can be.

When most people hear the name Francis of Assisi, a picture comes to mind of a gentle peacemaker who possessed a deep reverence for all creatures and who experienced God's love present in all the universe.

What most people do not know is that Francis was a survivor of severe physical and emotional abuse at the hands of his domineering father. I had been inspired by the love and gentleness of Francis for many years before realizing that it was our common bond as survivors that had unconsciously drawn me to learn more about him and his lifestyle. The manner in which he transformed his abusive past into a healed and loving life continues to offer me hope in my own process.

Francis separated from his family of origin in this manner. In his early twenties, when dragged before the bishop of Assisi by his irate father, Francis stripped off his clothes declaring he now had returned all that his father had ever given him. He then proclaimed, "No longer will I say my father, Pietro Bernadone, but our Father in heaven." True to his word, this young man was no longer called by the name given him by his parents at birth, John Bernadone. He became simply known as Francis, a new name reflecting his love of the French language and troubadour songs. Whenever my hope begins to fade or an ill-informed person declares that abused boys always grow up to become abusers, I remember the example of this adult survivor who grew up to become one of the most gentle and loving persons who ever lived.

A rationalization I have used to minimize the abuse is to say, "They never meant to harm me." Sexual abuse does not hurt any less because my abusers were in denial about their crime and continue to remain so. It is important for me as a survivor of incest to take my feelings seriously regarding my violation. As soon as I do this, I begin to take responsibility for my recovery. I no longer assume responsibility for my abusers. I am affected by my past but I am no longer controlled by my past.

It is often said in survivor circles, "Incest is not a family taboo–telling is." I believe that in recovery from incest, disclosure of the secret is always necessary. A survivor can tell what happened wherever he feels safe–with a therapist, friend, lover, or other survivors. With disclosure it is common for survivors to let go of unhealthy feelings of responsibility. This feeling of release happens over a period of time and often with repeated sharings and responses of acceptance, understanding, and validation by our listeners. Disclosing to other survivors is especially helpful for validating our memories, realizing we were treated unjustly, and separating from our abusers. Some would add that in addition to disclosure, confrontation with one's abuser is always necessary. My opinion is that it is best attempted only when the survivor feels secure enough within himself to fend off any additional abuse from the perpetrator, be it verbal, emotional, or physical abuse. And we only need to confront our abusers if <u>we</u> feel it would be helpful for us to do so.

I did confront my abusers–my mother who is alive and my father, uncle, and grandparents in the cemetery. I did it for one reason–to help myself in my recovery. I did so when I felt strong enough in myself so as not to take responsibility for my abusers or to accept more abuse from them (which was indeed offered). I was well-prepared before I attempted the confrontation.

There is no need to re-victimize ourselves. Having disclosed and/or confronted, we realize we will not disintegrate without the approval of the dysfunctional family that gave us birth. We are now free as adults to choose whether or not we desire to continue a relationship with any of these relatives. Unlike our childhood experience, we are now free to set our own boundaries of involvement.

12. Isolation and Intimacy

Is there a more humanly isolating experience than to be "physically intimate" with another without the presence of mutual love, dignity, and respect? I doubt if anyone knows such a poignant pain of isolation and rejection as we who are survivors of incest.

How devastating it is to have family members with whom I placed my trust and longed for true closeness, betray that trust with a dominating, smothering, invasive force they lied about and called "love."

A distorted relationship inflicted on us by wounded and abusive persons elicited a desire to isolate. Relationships were unsafe, painful and unrewarding. We were not motivated to develop relationships due to fear. It is risky to try again, to trust again. But risk I did. And open up I did. Life-giving relationships are the key to our healing reconnection with God, nature, others, and especially ourselves. I have been and continue to be more deeply loved.

Intimacy is a fantasy I chased for a long time–searching for the parents and friends I didn't have as a child. It is a dream of closeness without conflict, love without pain, complete acceptance without the slightest hint of rejection. I was willing to sell my freedom and expression of true feelings for such intimacy. Yet this fantasy was, in reality, a set-up for more rejection and victimization. I have now developed close relationships in my life. They are normal relationships with closeness _and_ conflict.

I am willing to accept and work through the conflicts that arise. I feel loved deeply, but I am also sensitive to rejection. When I perceive a snub or a put-down, I have learned to share my feelings and listen to the other person. Close relationships are not pain free. They are also _not_ based on pain. Sometimes I can differentiate between healthy and unhealthy relationships. An unhealthy relationship denies pain and forbids personal responsibility for feelings and actions. In short, it is isolating. It mirrors relationships experienced in my dysfunctional family of origin. Healthy relationships with real intimacy include real love and caring. Each person takes responsibility for his or her part in the relationship. Both people realize that the other has a darker side which can be uncaring and far from perfect. In isolating relationships (such as the incestuous family) personal darkness is denied (by the abuser) or blamed on the other (victim). My darkness is not a secret to myself or my friends. When intimate, I risk the vulnerability of my secret self–with all my beauty and all my warts.

Do I still get negative and fearful thoughts? Do I sometimes feel cut off and want to hide in work, food, or alcohol? Do I ever feel nobody cares? Yes. Yes. Yes. The difference is that today I realize that I have a choice. I can indulge in self pity, sulk, and isolate–proving I am no good, unlovable, and that the world is rotten. Or I can do something to get out of that "stinking thinking." I can let go of the shame.

I pick up the phone, call another survivor, and share my feelings. I go to a meeting of survivors as soon as I can, no matter what else is on my schedule. I ask my Higher Power (the God of my understanding, not of my victimization) to lift the burden. I pick up and read some survivor literature. I write or draw or sing or dance my feelings–and let them go. I ask the little boy inside me how he's feeling, listen to what he says and I respond with tender love and care. If I cannot contact another survivor, I call a friend or counselor with whom I have a bond and share my feelings. I ask someone with whom I feel secure for a hug, and I have a choice about explaining how I feel. I breathe deeply and slowly repeating an affirmation such as, "God wants only love for me" or "I am lovable and loving."

Pretty soon I've gained some perspective. I've moved from isolation to intimacy. Even if I am physically alone, I am intimate with and connected to myself. I realize I am a good and valuable part of the world. It feels good to be me. I still have problems but they do not overwhelm me.

I have been sharing with you some of my journal of recovery and hope. I am not perfect. I never will be. I do not need to be. But I am in the life process of recovery–from sickness to wellness, from victimization to surviving to thriving. I know that your recovery will not be identical to mine. However, I do hope my experiences will touch yours in whatever small way so that you may feel the strength and en-courage-ment in your healing process that I have felt from caring others in mine. We never have to feel alone again.

III

What You Can Do

You may have picked up this book to read because you are certain that you have been victimized by incest. You may be struggling to believe those eerie feelings and vague memories. You may feel like asserting, "Yes, I am a survivor." You may be feeling some doubts and may want to recant. "Perhaps my abuser or non-involved family member is right. I made it up or misunderstood." In my experience with survivors, such an inner struggle happens very often among us. It is almost as if the doubt of being a survivor is one of the signs of being a survivor. What can you do? First of all... Believe yourself, trust your feelings and experiences, no matter how clouded they may seem in your mind. And know that you are a good and special person, even if inner voices continue to argue to the contrary. As your (positive) voice becomes louder and stronger, the other (negative) voices will be drowned out.

As you begin to risk your feelings of having survived incest by sharing with trusted other(s), remember that most non-survivors may not understand our feelings as fully as other survivors. They have not experienced the abuse that we have. They may try to be very caring and understanding but after awhile they may ask, "Why don't you just put this all behind you?" Or, "Sure, terrible things happened to you, but you have got to stop thinking and talking about it—that's morbid. You're only depressing yourself."

This is my approach to incest: I know that I am a survivor of incest. It was a terrible, terrible thing to happen to me—an awful way to be brought up. But I am not under the authority of those unhealthy people anymore. I have survived incest and I am now dealing with its lifetime effects. I cannot deal with the effects by denying them or trying to put them all behind me. I cannot cope with them by continually bemoaning my misfortune and resenting my abusers. These approaches perpetuate my victimization by isolating me and my true feelings from others. I must take responsibility for myself in the here and now with all my history.

In my recovery at this time in my life, *Incest Survivor is a description of hope, not shame. Incest is a historical fact that I cannot alter. Incest is a personal violation. Incest has lifelong effects. Survivor describes the blessing of recovery. I still have times when I am anxious, scared, depressed, self-condemning, angry, or defensive BUT I am no longer a helpless victim unable to move out of these feelings. I am an incest <u>survivor</u>. I have tools of recovery.*

Incest is a very powerful trauma to have survived. The obvious implication is that we must have a very strong inner life force in order to have come through such a potent trauma. We were deprived of a normal childhood and a nurturing home because of the incest and accompanying family dysfunctions. We have a lot to recoup, a lot of damage from which to recover in body, mind, emotion, and spirit. I do not believe that any one path can encapsulate recovery from incest. This section discusses a variety of ways that I and others have employed in healing and growing as survivors. Perhaps some will be of benefit for you.

1. Traditional Talk Therapy

If you are considering therapy for incest or childhood abuse, it would benefit you to contact a psychologist, psychotherapist, pastoral counselor, or clinical social worker who is known to be sensitive, caring, and experienced in working with incest survivors. S/he may also be an incest survivor in recovery. Don't be afraid to look around, ask questions, and search out someone who is qualified and with whom you can establish a trusting relationship. Beware of a therapist who demands your complete blind trust from the start. Trust develops slowly. The therapist must earn your trust, so let him/her become trustworthy. We trust as we can. It cannot be forced or demanded—that is how we were hurt in the first place! And don't be afraid to leave a therapist whom you feel after a few sessions is not helpful or does not understand you. It is not healthy to work with a therapist whom you do not sense to be trustworthy, accepting, and compassionate. As a matter of fact, it can be counterproductive.

I entered therapy in my early twenties because I felt I was going crazy and did not know why. I thought my family of origin was good and loving. Incest was the furthest thing from my mind. Five years and a handful of therapists later I began openly to struggle with inner feelings of an abusive childhood. Many incest survivors initially enter therapy with other presenting problems. They may or may not remember the incest. An unspoken agreement can develop with the therapist that this topic will not be discussed. Often a person will successfully complete therapy for the stated problem only to return when frightening flashbacks, somatic symptoms, or pervasive feelings of fear and anxiety will not dissipate. What do you do when feelings or memories of incest arise during or after the therapy you initially entered for other problems? Believe yourself. Trust your feelings. Try to share your feelings with the therapist. You may feel intense pain, anger, fear, and sorrow, but know that the healing process has begun. The time has come to face the abusive past. The only way out is through.

This will not be possible to achieve if you have a therapist who does not honor your feelings and memories or who agrees with you when you say, "Maybe it didn't really happen," calling your memories fantasy or projection of unfulfilled wishes. It can be hard for us to challenge therapists because we don't want to lose them as we once lost our parents when they failed to protect us from incest or disbelieved us afterwards. But to stay with such a therapist is to stay a victim. When I had initially shared with a counselor the feelings of being molested by an uncle, he tried to explain it away as a non-factual memory. Survivor after survivor has shared a similar story. This is especially true for men because society perpetuates the falsehood that males are strong, aggressive, initiators—and not victims. Society tries to silence its male victims in shame, saying: "Real men aren't victimized. Are you saying you're not a real man?" And if the perpetrator was female: "What man wouldn't want a woman to lie with him? What's wrong with you" Aren't you a real man?" The truth is that real men were (and continue to be) victimized by unhealthy persons in positions of power and authority. We were helpless and dependent children when the abuse happened, needing to believe the adult was OK even at our own expense. *We male survivors are gay, straight, and bisexual, but it was not our sexuality that invited abuse—we were raped.*

And when the rapist was our own mother, we were devastated, not gratified.

I was fortunate regarding therapists. I eventually found a psychologist who accepted me and believed me when I needed and wanted to protect my fantasy family by rejecting and disbelieving myself. He was my advocate when I was trying to be my mother's advocate. I tried to convince my therapist that I was the liar my mother said I was. When I hear other male survivors describe how they had to convince their therapist that they were really victimized, I realize what a strange crime incest is: The perpetrator's word is taken as the primary evidence of what happened and the victim is put on trial as the criminal. Fortunately, increased publicity has heightened public awareness about the reality and devastation of incest as well as its frequency of occurrence. More and more sensitive and trained therapists are available to assist the survivor in the healing process.

Talk therapy is one of the avenues of healing for the incest survivor. I have needed much more in my recovery from my traumatic childhood. Perhaps the greatest help I received after the strides made in individual therapy came from self-help groups.

2. Self-Help Groups

Individual therapy with a qualified, compassionate person can be of great assistance in the healing process. However, it frequently does not go far enough for most survivors. The office of a trusted therapist can be a safe place to share, yet it can also remind survivors of some aspects of the relationship in which abuse was experienced. What is shared is shared in secret between two persons. The person with whom one shares is perceived by the survivor to be more powerful. The survivor has to pay for the attention given. And at times when the survivor may feel like screaming out or physically expressing (e.g., punching a bag) powerful feelings that arise, he may feel constrained or encouraged to hold them back because others (in neighboring offices) might hear and become upset. The survivor may expect that someone might become upset with either himself or the therapist and then alter his behavior in a familiar, protective way.

More complete healing can begin when the survivor is able to share the secret with peers and feel their acceptance, validation, and understanding. Many survivors have come to an awareness of our victimization through participation in a 12 Step recovery group. Sometimes a tentative disclosure will be made in groups such as Alcoholics Anonymous, Overeaters Anonymous, Narcotics Anonymous, and Adult Children of Alcoholics Anonymous. Other times, survivors attend meetings without speaking. I believe the number of survivors using 12-step programs is substantial. Some persons come to the awareness of incest, perhaps for the first time, with the aid of one of these fellowships. They may have sought these groups for other acknowledged problems first. Once they experience 12-step recovery as beneficial in one area, it is logical for them to seek a similar recovery process for their incest. Some survivors seek out 12-step recovery programs encouraged to do so by another survivor, a book, a movie, or a television report on child abuse.

Incest Survivors Anonymous (ISA) and Survivors of Incest Anonymous (SIA) are two such 12 -step programs in which individual groups are rapidly forming throughout this country and abroad. (See Resources) Some are same sex groups and others are mixed. I believe both types of groups are necessary in recovery. Same sex groups may initially feel safer. In time we come to understand emotionally that it was our abusers' sick attitudes that fostered our fear of persons of either sex and kept us apart. Together, men and women survivors are empowered to own their unique strengths and individual gifts.

There are other types of survivor groups which can be helpful. For instance, I participate in a monthly men's discussion group which focuses on a different survivor issue at each meeting (e.g., sexuality, relationships, depression, self-healing, and so forth). What is important is to choose a safe, nurturing environment in which you feel comfortable, supported, validated and open to growth. If a group does not feel helpful or feels abusive, you have a right to say so and choose to leave—a choice that was not available to you in your dysfunctional family of origin. Therapy groups including those led by a recovering survivor therapist, can be very helpful. These groups can provide you with some of the dynamics of a healthy family. They also encourage you to acknowledge and express feelings in a safe and caring atmosphere.

There may not be any survivor groups in your area open to men. There were none where I live until I started one. During the interim, my lifeline of recovery was through incest survivor-journals which serve as a written forum for survivor sharing—a sort of self-help group by mail. I would like to refer you to the Resources section in the back of the book to read about resources which continue to be a great source of support and encouragement to me. Individual therapy is enhanced by group support, acceptance, and validation. Group and individual processes compliment each other and foster growth and new life.

3. Bodywork and Non-Traditional Healing

Many of us dissociated from our bodies at the time of incest in order to survive. In order to reconnect now as survivors, we need to feel safe and secure in our bodies and to honor our physical selves with care and love. I find that our twentieth century culture offers little in terms of healing the body. Psychotherapy primarily focuses on talking and medicine is largely a combination of drug therapies and surgery. These approaches do not revere the body. Meanwhile, the word massage conjures up images of prostitution available through massage parlors. There are nonetheless some healing and legitimate types of bodywork which can be powerful recovery avenues for survivors.

Physical exercise is perhaps the most wholesome and available form of bodywork. Doing aerobic exercise—be it walking, running, swimming, bicycling, hiking—on a daily basis, can allow us to feel the parameters of our physical selves. It offers the advantage of no physical contact when survivors don't feel ready for physical contact. In addition, exercise brings conscious awareness to your body. I cannot even wiggle my toes if I am out of my body and up near the ceiling—as during my abuse. But if I can at least wiggle my toes, I know I am in my body. Those who have dissociated from their bodies will understand what I mean.

Aerobic exercise requires us to breathe deeply and regularly. Many of us automatically constrict our lungs and abdomen when feeling tense or anxious. We hold in fear and anxiety in the same way we did during the assault. Exercise allows us to release tension, to breathe, and to relax our muscles. The repetitive nature of running or walking can also serve as a type of mantra to open our spirits to meditation.

Massage requires we trust another person with our body. We have to feel entitled to tell that person to stop at any point in the massage if we become frightened or uncomfortable. The person does not have the right to touch us wherever we say we do not want to be touched. Touching, tickling, and stroking were once weapons of invasion used against us by our attackers. Through therapeutic massage we can learn how touch can be used gently and firmly to heal our physical and emotional wounds. We can experience a relaxing of muscles, a release of stress and tension, and a pleasurable bodily sensation that does not seek or demand a sexual payoff.

Therapeutic Touch was developed in the nursing profession by Dolores Krieger (1979) to facilitate healing in others through a process which combines meditation with non-invasive touch. The results of this type of bodywork include relaxation, a sense of well-being, and a connectedness with one's own body and the universe. I became a practitioner and teacher of Therapeutic Touch before remembering my violation at the hands of mother and father. In retrospect, I believe that I wanted to teach the hundreds of health care professionals I worked with how to use touch in a loving and healing way—instead of the manipulative and invasive manner that I had long ago endured. What a wonderful revelation to learn and experience touch as it was meant to be—for love and healing and connection—rather than abuse, separation, and isolation.

Reiki Healing is another touch therapy that involves a gentle laying-on-of-hands. Because it does not involve rubbing or stroking, it is less reminiscent of abusive touch than some types of massage. Receiving and giving Reiki with trusted others has helped me love and appreciate my body as good and lovable.

Rolfing is a deep, physical form of bodywork through which the bodyworker massages the body's myofascial tissue to help the body return to its natural alignment with gravity (Rolf, 1978). The goal of rolfing is to help the body to let go of unhealthy ways of holding oneself (rooted in past responses to life). Five years ago I knew I was holding a lot of pain in my body. Through rolfing with a strong and sensitive woman rolfer, much of the pain of my inner child was able to come to the surface and cry out for help. Rolfing is a deeply intensive form of bodywork and it is useful to have a good support system in place if engaging in this kind of bodywork.

Acupuncture and acupressure are derived from traditional Chinese methods of healing with or without the use of needles. Balance of the elements within oneself and in relation to the world is its basic goal. Healing and wholeness are promoted through a balanced energy flow throughout the body. The procedure is relatively non-invasive and pain free.

I have benefited from each of the above processes in my healing journey. This is not meant to be an exhaustive list of healing modalities for the body, but a sampling of what has been helpful to me. For those of us who experienced a severe dissociation from our body as a result of incest, some program of bodywork can be essential for reclaiming our bodies, becoming whole, and living a fuller life.

4. Imagery, Visualization, Meditation, Art

I was tempted to call this section Right Brain Techniques because they go beyond mere logic to a deeper openness to the heart itself (oneself). We have often invested so much of our energy into covering up and protecting. The following techniques reverse that process by focusing on creative imagination and expression. *Be assured that the most destructive forces of incest we endured are no match in the long run for the creative forces of our spirit.*

Imagery includes inner word and thought pictures. "I am a lovable child" is an example of a word picture (affirmation) you can cherish in your mind many times a day. Seeing yourself as a lovable little boy is a thought picture. Having an actual photograph of yourself as a child that you can look at with love and care—which you can easily carry around with you in your wallet—is a gentle way to keep on loving the child who is very much a part of you. These practices may feel uncomfortable and difficult at first. The snapshots of the innocent you, may bring back the pain so brutally suffered. Practiced regularly, new doors of love and positive self-parenting are opened.

Visualization is a way of seeing yourself in your mind as lovable and free to live. You may not yet feel spontaneous enough to let your playful child romp through a mud puddle—but you can visualize yourself doing so and having a blast. You can practice visualizing the world as the loving and safe place it was created to be, and then test out your visions in supportive places.

Meditation is a quieting of mind and spirit. This is not easy for many of us whose minds are usually used to racing a mile a minute, planning, anticipating, fearing. We can learn to trust in a Higher Power who wants only love for us. You may consciously choose to place your anxious thoughts aside for a while, realizing you can pick them up later. Try sitting in a comfortable, quiet place. Breathe deeply. Relax and close your eyes. Perhaps you will choose a one word mantra to focus your mind: "Love," "God," "Peace," etc. Don't think about it. Simply breathe it until you are open and at peace. Take your twenty minute meditation by jogging or sitting in a hot bath. Through meditation you can discover ever new places of safety within yourself and feel more deeply connected with your outer world in lifegiving ways. Meditation is empowering and helpful in letting go of your former lifestyle of hypervigilance and learning the ways of serenity.

Art is a generic term I use for creative self-expression. This is an especially important mode of expression for those of us whose inner child was violated at a pre-verbal stage, either in infancy or early childhood. Drawing/painting is a wonderful way of externalizing feelings, especially when you feel them constricting you and have no words to express them. The aesthetic quality of your drawing is not of prime importance. Getting the feelings out and being able to see them symbolically on paper (even if you don't understand their meaning) is itself a healing. For other survivors, sculpting or modeling accomplishes much the same thing.

Music, poetry, and dance are other freeing forms of self expression. Music has an impact on most of us. Songs touch inner places of sadness, hurt, anger, or serenity and can stimulate memories. Music can be used to reinforce positive feelings or as a backdrop for meditation. Songs written by and for survivors have a healing and unifying effect when sung at a retreat or conference.

I love to sing full-voiced, though I shied away from it for many years. Singing helps me process my feelings. Others who are musically inclined say much the same for playing a musical instrument. I draw poorly and have a good singing voice, but each is helpful in my recovery because each helps externalize my feelings and open the door to my heart in a different way.

Dance is another wonderful bodily expression of feeling. Because of the incest we often feel awkward, uncomfortable, and guilty in our bodies. And yet at times there is a beautiful dancer imprisoned within, longing to be set free. Many survivors feel no inclination to dance, yet give themselves permission to move, so they can experience a sense of well-being through movement.

Creative writing is a powerful tool for survivors. Poetry, prose, letters and short stories give us a form into which the words of our feelings and experiences can flow. Survivor journals, a few of which are listed in Resources, provide an invaluable way to share our souls.

The avenues of imagination and art I have singled out represent our creative spirits in both inner vision and outer expression. Ideally we strive for a balance of the two in recovery. Some of us who are more introverted or extraverted by nature will choose those creative outputs that suit our primary inclinations. Incest was a form of brainwashing which distorted our perceptions and responses to the world. *Now we have tools which help us gain a healthier sense of self and en-courage us to express our gifted, creative spirit in relationship with the world of which we are a valued part.*

5. Connecting with Nature

Incest isolated us from ourselves and our-world. We were made to feel different, no good and alien to this world. In recovery we learn that each of us is a worthwhile and valuable part of nature. Some survivors consider nature a special place in which to connect with God. Others identify nature as their Higher Power. Whatever the case, nature is a valuable aspect of our healing process. We are born of nature and no matter how much we may protest, we are a part of nature during life and nature will receive us once again in death.

The world of air, plants, animals, and minerals knows what it is like to be raped and abused by humans who have not learned reverence for the earth. At times the elements of nature have been our first confidants and comforters before we had the courage to tell other humans that we too have been raped. We are a part of nature. Nature understands. Some of us were abused and betrayed by our parents. We mourn the loss and sometimes feel like orphans in this world. At such times nature can teach us that no mere human could ever be our true parent. We are born of a Parent much more loving and faithful. Otherwise, how could we ever have survived the devastation we've been through?

Hundreds of years ago a simple, gentle man named Francis of Assisi wrote a beautiful song about the presence of the divine in all creation. He called his song, the Canticle of the Creatures, and in it referred to Brother Sun, Sister Moon, Mother Earth, Brother Fire, Sister Water, Brother Air, and even Sister Death. He was a survivor of childhood abuse who through his healing process learned how valuable and precious every element of the universe is, and that all creation is filled with God's presence. He found that reverence and respect is the true nature of the universe. He became transformed from an isolated, abused young man into a person who felt the full loving presence of his Higher Power.

I've gotten a glimpse of that type of view whenever I've taken a walk down the street to a nearby brook. The sound of the flowing water has a way of washing away the feelings of stress that so easily multiply within me. I can feel the warmth of the sun, breathe deeply the fresh air, listen to the chattering birds, feel the squishy earth beneath my feet and realize that I am an intimate part of all this. Connect with nature. Open to the healing love of the universe all around you. You may experience it more powerfully near the ocean or on a mountain top; in the woods or on a lake. But it is also in the tree growing in an otherwise concrete jungle, in the open sky beyond the sky-scrapers, and in the faces of those nameless persons you meet on city streets. It happens everywhere. My first teacher of Therapeutic Touch used to connect with those inner places of nature and serenity where all is perceived as one, and channel peace while riding the subway. As you are able to connect with nature, remember your heritage as a beloved child. Your heritage is much deeper and higher than your abusers led you to believe. We have survived. We are destined to thrive.

6. Retreats, Conferences, and Workshops

When we survivors get together with those who love us, we call these events gatherings, workshops, conferences, or retreats. What they are in reality, are times to come together for mutual support, encouragement, ongoing healing, and continued hope. Conferences may have speakers who share of their personal recovery from incest and/or their professional work with survivors. There are usually times for survivor-only sharing for men, women, and mixed groups. Sometimes these days are goal-oriented, exploring for instance, new modes of self expression or looking at recovery as an individual and group process. They represent opportunities for continued learning through interaction, reflection, and discussion.

These conferences are not sessions for group self-pity, bitterness, or vengeance. Such attitudes keep us locked into the victim role, reacting to a perceived hostile world. We gather as persons in process—wounded yet being healed, victimized in the past but learning to live as survivors in the present. We gather to affirm our goodness and disown the shame that was imposed on us by our victimizers. Our coming together unmasks many of the falsehoods about incest: that all victims become sex offenders, that only women are victimized, that only men initiate incest, that incest is isolated and rare, that the abused child asks for sex and enjoys it, and that survivors fabricate incestuous histories to blame others for their unhappiness or to elicit pity. *We are justifiably angry and outraged at such lies—and we shall not be silenced!*

Incest survivor conferences provide an excellent opportunity for advocacy and public consciousness raising. We are evidence of the estimates that there are millions of adult survivors: perhaps 40 million in this country alone. Current estimates state that at least one in three girls and no less than one in six boys are involved in some form of forced sexual experience with an adult before the age of 18. This means that most survivors are still suffering, or trudging a solitary path to healing. There are also millions of children and adults in dependency positions who continue to be victimized. We stand as a public witness that they are not alone, and that there is hope and healing beyond the victimization. We search out ways of stirring public support for advocacy so that intervention may be given to the innocent who continue to be abused.

Women have done the ground breaking work in organizing extended gatherings for survivors to provide mutual support, encouragement, and healing. More recently, weekend retreats and workshops are being organized for male survivors of incest. A feeling of safety is enhanced on these weekends by admitting only survivors who have not become perpetrators. Each person must be willing to abide by certain guidelines concerning respect for oneself and the boundaries of others. The leaders are often therapists or recovering survivors who are experienced in working with survivors.

Despite the external safeguards, everyone who attends is reminded of their right to say "no" to whatever does not feel right. Choosing to participate on a weekend, like choosing a therapist or a group, always comes back to your evaluation of what is or is not helpful for you in your recovery.

What are the benefits of these weekend retreats/workshops for men as incest survivors? It can be validating to hear other survivors, many of whom we are meeting for the first time. It is empowering to share feelings, doubts, fears, and experiences similar to our own. We realize we are not crazy or liars; our abusers are the ones who betrayed and deceived us. The sheer fact that so many survivors come together to share at a deeply personal level is a source of encouragement when we often feel so alone in our day-to-day lives. The variety of persons who have survived the devastation of incest and struggle with many of the same issues enlightens us to the reality that there are few (if any) significant differences in healing for men and women of different races and creeds, young and old, gay/lesbian and straight survivors. *We become empowered by the sense that we are partners in healing overcoming our common enemy—the devastation of incest. We feel strengthened and encouraged by our involvement with so many others who understand the depth of our hurt and rage and who share hope in the healing journey.*

7. Prayer and Solitude

The damage we suffered as victims of incest was physical, mental, and emotional. Our recovery is rooted in the Spirit, whether we call that spiritual force God, Higher Power, Love, Healing Energy, Jesus, Nature, or something else entirely. Whatever we call our Higher Power, it is different from the oppressive, judgmental "God" of our misunderstanding which was distorted by incest and often by overreligious parents as well.

Because religion and a punishing God are so often closely linked with our incestuous past and threats against telling, some of us have rejected religion altogether as a means of contact with a Higher Power. We find God within ourselves, in trusted friends, in our survivor group, and in nature. In these types of prayer we connect with the life force we need in order to live, to grow, to receive and give love.

Other survivors have kept religion but changed Gods. No longer do we believe in a Higher Power cast in the destructive image of our perpetrator—a phony Higher Power whom we experienced as controlling, secretive, vindictive, domineering, and abusive. Instead we have found our true Higher Power at the center of our being and reflected in others who honor life and prefer honesty to secrecy. Prayer is the open line of communication with our Higher Power whom we can experience in our own hearts and with each other.

"But for the grace of God" is a slogan commonly heard in 12-step recovery. The grace of God, the care of a Higher Power, can be experienced by survivors in a number of ways. It may be that stranger at a meeting sharing exactly what you needed to hear that night. It may be a friend who calls to say he or she was led to pray for you the other day—and it turns out to be the exact time you first disclosed. Grace for us is a vision that sees the forces of love and life in a world that once seemed to hold only betrayal and devastation.

As you journey on the path from victimization to recovery, you will begin to appreciate the value of solitude. Solitude is not the frightened child's silence or hiding under the bed covers with all your clothes on or being unnoticed whenever you are in a group of people. Solitude is a part of recovery in which we can enjoy being by ourselves without feeling isolated. It is a chance to meet our Higher Power in quiet and to fill the inner emptiness that seemed even too deep for God. It is an opportunity to value and enjoy the gift of self alone, so that we might more fully value and enjoy ourselves with others. Prayer and solitude are vital elements in daily recovery.

8. Nurturing the Child Within

Imagine for a minute being a very young child and having to take care of two children who are lonely, hurt, angry, unhappy, and refuse to talk with each other about how they really feel. Now imagine that these two emotionally disturbed children are a lot bigger and stronger than you. Although you are only a child yourself, these big kids look to you to meet their emotional needs. If you don't do what they want, they will punish you or make you feel guilty for not taking better care of them. Many survivors called these big kids, mother and father. We grew up in a dysfunctional family, were deprived of childhoods, and had severe emotional demands placed on us—in addition to the sexual abuse we suffered. *We grew up to become caretakers, but did not know how to care for the child within ourselves.*

Society places a lot of expectations on how adults ought to act. Yet many of us have been acting adult since early childhood: cooking, cleaning, putting drunk parents to bed, making excuses for them to teachers and friends, trying to fill their emotional needs, being their sexual partners. Play and spontaneity were often missing from our lives. Our bodies grew large, but the child who longs for unconditional love and care is still very much alive inside of us.

Recovery is exemplified by the man who carries a cuddly teddy bear and bought himself flowers as a surprise just the other day. It is the woman who remembers herself with a special gift for her birthday and comforts herself with the doll she used to cry herself to sleep with as a frightened girl. Our love-objects remind us to cuddle and nurture ourselves and to listen to the child within who has many feelings to share, but is often afraid. You are the protective and loving mother and father that your inner child was deprived of by your natural parents. "What is my little boy saying to me?", is a question I ask myself whenever I feel compulsive, anxious, fearful, joyful, or sad. Our feelings come primarily from the child within. Carrying snapshots of yourself in your wallet, especially around the age of your abuse, can be a reminder that you are the first child you need to love (even if you have natural children of your own). Look at the photo. See how precious and innocent you were. NO ONE HAD THE RIGHT TO VIOLATE YOU. Allow yourself-whatever you may feel. Love yourself now as your abusers never could. You are worth all the love in the world!

A few months ago I was at a 12 Step evening of reflection. We had been sharing our stories in small groups and I had shown the pictures of my child during my sharing. The group leader then asked us to go apart for a few minutes and pray for the other persons in our group however we experienced God loving them. One woman came back and shared her prayer with me. "I believe there are no time barriers in prayer, so I just went to you and saw you as a beautiful three year- old. I picked you up in my arms and held you in God's love." We all cried, and I felt deeply loved. I have done the same for myself many times since then. It helps. Sometimes in church I voice a prayer for healing for a little boy from an abusive home. Only I know that I am that boy. And the prayer extends to all the little ones who continue to remain helpless in the face of incestuous victimization. Nurture your child. Every day. He is beautiful and precious. Love heals.

9. Opening to Love and Forgiveness

It sounds almost strange to talk about opening to love and forgiveness, because we survivors tend to be people who from our childhood were always quick to love others, forgiving or minimizing their harmful actions. When we got in touch with our hurt and rage over the injustices and violations done to us, we may have resented those we felt betrayed by and yet needed to love. Some of us swore we would never forgive.

When we hear a phrase like "opening to love and forgiveness" we may fail to see that *love and forgiveness is the gift that is long overdue ourselves.* For many of us love became a one way street of giving and giving. Often we were incapable or reluctant to receive love because of our previous disappointments and betrayal. One must be human and vulnerable in order to receive love. We became reluctant or afraid of love because those from whom we most needed love as children had responded with a mixture of love and rejection—abusive love. To open to love is to open to the possibility of rejection. To become human and vulnerable is to open to the awareness of our feelings regarding incest—hurt, rage, rejection, betrayal, fear, helplessness, confusion, even despair. Opening to love is scary yet the only way out is through. We first risk tentatively in places that appear to be safe and protected—with a close friend, a therapist, another survivor. And we slowly, cautiously experience the wonder of love. We may feel strengthened. Our tentative first steps lead to an en-courage-ment to risk ourselves more fully in healthy relationships. All our caretaking of the past never won for us what we really desired. The risk of a gradual opening to love in healthy, trusting relationships, allows us to be gifted with the awareness that we have been precious and lovable persons all along. Each of us must decide if it is worth the risk to find out.

As I see it, forgiveness is an act of love based on self-acceptance that allows me to trust God to be God, to accept personal responsibility for my own life, and to let go (when ready) of unhealthy feelings of vengeance or resentment that keep me emotionally bound to another. Forgiveness is a lifetime process and it cannot be rushed. *You are the primary object of your forgiveness, and God is its source deep within you.*

You may have tried to forgive or excuse your abusers when you were children or early in your remembering. However, this attempt to stop the pain and anger is usually accomplished at the cost of our deeper feelings of betrayal and violation, which we may then turn against ourselves. *Self-acceptance is the essence of forgiveness.* We did not experience unconditional love and acceptance as children. *We now need to soak in it, like a long, hot, soothing bath. It may be many months or years of soaking before we are ready to move into the next step.*

Accepting responsibility for your own life comes in conjunction with letting go and letting God. You may have many deep hurts and resentments to express and process with your Higher Power before you are ready to trust a new understanding of a loving God. Allow yourself the time and space to trust as well as the support of a program sponsor or spiritual advisor to walk with you.

"Do I have to forgive the perpetrator?" If you are asking this question, the answer is "No, not now anyway." What you will need to do is to give expression and release to the feelings of hurt, anger, rage, resentment, sorrow, etc. which have been stifling and suffocating you for such a long time. This can be facilitated through disclosures to supportive others and when and if appropriate for you, confrontation with the abusers and their accomplices.

Confrontation takes many forms. Some people do it directly; others indirectly. I confronted one live abuser and two dead ones. Letters you send or don't, audio or video-tapes you make to send or not, role-playing, and other expressions are also ways of confronting. *Confrontation is for you the survivor, not for the abuser.* You have complete control about "how" you confront.

As we heal, we grow to love and accept ourselves more fully. We no longer choose to abuse ourselves by holding in or denying these powerful feelings. Expressing them directly to our abusers can make us feel empowered. I believe that hanging onto our strong feelings of resentment, hurt, and blame is not an act of consideration but an advanced form of emotional dependency on the very persons who had abused us. Such dependency was needed when we were children, but we need it no longer. We are responsible for our own lives now. And we trust in a power deep within ourselves who offers strength, hope, and guidance.

You have now arrived at the doorway to true forgiveness. You will no longer need to hurt yourself, but hold only love and respect for yourself. You will not need to resent or rage about the past, yet you will respond to present acts of victimization directed at you or others with anger, outrage and appropriate action. A deep and abiding trust in a loving Higher Power will be the serenity that sustains you.... One day at a time I continue to work my program of recovery in the hope of walking through that doorway.

10. Carrying the Message of Hope

It is not coincidental that I have put reaching out to others at the end of suggestions for what you can do to begin to recover from incest. Many of us survivors would want to jump from the initial awareness that we were somehow violated, into an immediate caretaking of others. We are so used to being caretakers. This is what 12 Step program people call "two stepping" because we jump from our admission of powerlessness over incest to that part of Step 12 about carrying the message to others. Without attending to our feelings, however, helping others is premature and an avoidance of the heart of the healing process. Many of us have consciously or unconsciously avoided dealing with ourselves as incest victims and survivors by becoming helping professionals. Most of our energy becomes directed towards others. We attempt to get self-worth through and avoid abuse by helping and pleasing others whom we perceive as more deserving. Caretaking has short-term, not long-term rewards.

Carrying the message to others who are still suffering and those who are in the process of healing is an essential part of recovery for us all. It goes hand-in-hand with the other aspects of the healing process. And it is included in the 12th Step adapted from Alcoholics Anonymous (1952) for use by incest survivors: "Having had a spiritual awakening as a result of these steps, we tried to carry this message to [incest victims/survivors], and to practice these principles in all our affairs. "

The first part of this step asserts the spiritual transformation that occurs in moving from victim to survivor and includes the work of the first eleven steps. It involves remembering what recovery entails:

- We accept the reality of what happened to us (incest)

- We acknowledge our powerlessness over it

- We recognize there is a Higher Power who loves us

- We seek out the guidance of Higher Power

- We begin to take inventory about what happened in our past

- We accept whatever feelings and memories that may come

- We become open to love and compassion for ourselves and for whatever we had to do in order to survive a hostile and abusive environment

- We open to forgiveness in ourselves and in our relationships
- We continue to employ all the tools we learn
- We take opportunities available to us for healing, growth, and advocacy
- We accept the responsibility of shaping a new life as survivors

No doubt about it, as a result of working the steps my life continues to change. I am still a helping professional, but my priority is living a lifestyle that is loving and life-giving for me. For some survivors, growth has meant leaving a helping profession or whatever work they did. All of us however, view our lives, relationships, and work through new eyes—those of a child now freed to love and be loved and of an adult empowered to live. We find ourselves moving from survivors to thrivers.

We have spoken the long-forbidden secret and have moved from darkness to light, from shame to self-respect. This is the point where we choose to carry the message of hope to others. We are freed to share out of our experience, strength, and hope with others who are struggling with the long-term effects of incest. Surviving incest is an ongoing process in which we experience healing, growth and progress. We do not become perfect people. Our wounds continue to heal; the scars remain. We reach out to others in compassion and thereby enhance our own growth.

Some of us have embraced a 12-Step way of living in order to counteract the harmful effects of incest for ourselves and to become empowered advocates for others. Obviously this is what has been very helpful for me — but it is one way, not the only way, to freedom from the bondage of incest. Every day more and more male survivors are speaking out on our own behalf. We are finding a variety of means for healing, networking, and advocacy. Some of these possibilities are listed in the Resource section of this book. I urge you to keep on trying various avenues in this regard until you find what works best for you.

And through it all please remember that the victimization can and must end. You are not alone. Together we can.

Afterword

Reflections on Myths, Monsters, and Remembering My True Nature

The following reflections constitute the *short form* of this book.

In recovering from the devastation of incest we must deal with some formidable denial, both in society and in our abusive families. I address the first form of denial as "myths," and the second as inner "monsters"—what Dr. Carl Jung called the consciously unacceptable or "shadow" side of reality. When we can break these onerous taboos of secrecy which surround incest, we are freed to acknowledge our heritage as valued, lovable and precious members of this universe.

MYTHS ABOUT MEN

These are some "myths" about men and incest:

- Men can be abusers but not victims of incest.

- Male survivors become sex offenders.

- A boy would never be incestuously victimized by his mother, grandmother, sister, aunt, or other female relative.

- Male survivor issues are different from those of female survivors.

The truth is:

Society's demands on the male victim often humiliate him into keeping silence—denying the abuse even to himself.

While perhaps 80-90% of child molesters and 50% of rapists were themselves sexually abused as children, the statistics do not work in reverse. As more and more non-offending male survivors are speaking out, this hurtful lie is being exposed.

Many boys are incestuously violated and betrayed by female offenders. Incest does not respect gender in its perpetration: men and women initiate with male and female victims.

There are few, if any, significant differences in the recovery issues faced by men and women survivors. Whatever fear we may have of each other was implanted in us by the persons who abused us. Same sex groups and men-and-women groups are both needed for healing and recovery. It works. Together we are empowered.

Monsters don't run away scared just because I said "Monsters." That's what Mummy and Daddy did. They "loved" me, but they said there were no such things as monsters. Boy, were they wrong!

Mummy and Daddy were good people, but they didn't know how to take care of their monsters—and I really got hurt. Monsters live inside everybody. They can be big and scary. Real scary. When I was little I had no one to protect me from monsters. Mummy and Daddy said they would- -then they said monsters were just make believe. But they hurt my wee wee and they hurt me between my legs and my rear end. And they yelled at me (screamed at me) and at each other. They broke things, scared me to death, and said they'd kill me for being "bad."

Mummy and Daddy used to cuddle me and play with me. We used to have lots of fun together and laugh—until the monsters came. When the monsters came and hurt me and I tried to tell Mummy and Daddy, they got real scared and mad and said in a mad voice: "Stop making those things up you bad boy!" So I got scared and got real quiet so they wouldn't be mad at me anymore. When I grew up I drank a lot and ate a lot but the monsters wouldn't go away. They had been inside Mummy and Daddy. Now they were inside me.

I live with a big man now who's a good Mummy and Daddy for me. He knows all about monsters and we can talk about them whenever we need to or whenever we get scared. I guess the Mummy and Daddy I had when I was little didn't know anything about monsters and were too scared of them. But even if I get scared now, I don't have to stay that way.

The first thing we do is not pretend the monsters aren't there. Monsters look big and mean but they can't hurt us anymore. We talk to them ("Hello, Monster, what's your name?"). Monsters usually are real mad and hurt a lot. So we take them out for long walks, or have them do backwards somersaults down grassy hills, see if they want to play with one of our toys, or give them a little something to eat,(They love animal crackers). Don't use big words with monsters and don't let them bully you. Remember, you have the right to say "No" and "Stop."

Mummy and Daddy used to be afraid they were monsters. I grew up afraid I was the real monster. We were all wrong. Now I know what they never did. I say, "Monster, you can't fool me. Mummy and Daddy weren't monsters. I'm sure not a monster. Only monsters can be monsters, and they live inside people. You can't hurt me anymore, and you can't make me hurt anyone either—not even myself. Now have an animal cracker and be quiet. It's time for me to have some fun!"

Remember Your Heritage

Little one so filled with tears

How beautiful you are!

Born in time

You are so much more

Than the child whom most see.

Remember your heritage.

Bruised and battered and broken

Are not the parents of your spirit.

Earth bore you from her gentle womb

Air fathered you in sustaining love

E'er before you knew betrayal

By the surrogates who raised you.

Remember your noble birth.

A Higher Power than any flesh and blood

Could conceive

Forms the center of your being

Cradling your inner child with love

And tenderness.

Remember your divine spark.

The sun who enlightens your day

Is the brother within you named Courage

Who brings to light

The dark secrets of your abusers.

Water who cleanses and purifies

Is your sister within named Healing

Who brings peace and refreshment

To your troubled soul.

Remember your family line.

Incest is not my father

Nor abuse my mother at all.

They were a heritage of people

Not big enough or little enough

To be my parents.

I remember my heritage:

It is of nature.

I remember my lineage:

It is most human.

I celebrate my origin:

I am of God.

Resources

SURVIVORS OF INCEST ANONYMOUS

A 12-Step fellowship for survivors of sexual abuse with an international meeting directory and survivor literature.

SIA World Service Office
P.O. Box 21817
Baltimore, MD   21222

INCEST SURVIVORS ANONYMOUS

A 12-Step fellowship for survivors of sexual abuse with an international meeting directory and survivor literature.

ISA World Service Office
P.O. Box 5613
Long Beach, CA   90805

P.L.E.A.

An organization founded by a male survivor for non-offending male survivors of childhood physical, sexual, emotional abuse and neglect. Referrals, resources, and a quarterly newsletter.

P.L.E.A.
Zia Road — Box 22
Santa Fe, NM   87505
(505) 982-9184

SAFER SOCIETY PROGRAM AND PRESS

Directed by Honey Fay Knopp who has been an advocate of male survivors for over 35 years. She has done extensive work with survivors and offenders of both sexes. Telephone referrals, networking information, publications.

The Safer Society Program
RR1 — Box 24-B
Orwell, VT   05760
(802) 897-7541

CHILDHLEP USA

National Hotline directed by Dan Sexton, an outspoken survivor, therapist, and advocate for victims and survivors of childhood abuse. National child abuse hotline for information and referrals.

> CHILDHELP USA
> 1345 El Centro Avenue
> P.O. Box 630
> Hollywood, CA   90028
> (1-800)   422-4453

LOOKING UP

Based in Maine, this survivor-founded organization for women and men includes specialized services for male survivors such as literature, referral resources, backpacking trips, and an annual gathering. Free bi-monthly mailings include resource information and a survivor literary and art magazine, The Looking Up Times.

> "LOOKING UP"
> P.O. Box K
> Augusta, ME   04332
> (207)   626-3402

INCEST SURVIVOR INFORMATION EXCHANGE

A quarterly publication which provides a forum for male and female survivors to share prose, poetry, art and resource information.

> I.S.I.E.
> P.O. Box 3399
> New Haven, CT   06515

Suggested Readings

Bass, E. & Davis, L. (1988). The courage to heal: A guide for women survivors of child sexual abuse. New York: Harper and Row.

Bass, E. (1983). I never told anyone. New York: Harper & Row.

Bear, E., & Dimock, P. T. (1987). Adults molested as children: A survivors manual for women and men. Orwell, VT: Safer Society Press.

Bear, E. & Dimock, P. T., (1988). Adults molested as children: A survivor's manual for men and women. Orwell, VT: Safer Society Press.

Black, C. (1982). It will never happen to me. Denver, CO:-Medical Administration Company.

Braun, B. G., (Ed.), (1986). Treatment of multiple personality disorder. Washington, DC: American Psychiatric Press.

Butler, S. (1978). Conspiracy of silence: The trauma of incest. San Francisco: New Glide Publications.

Caruso, B. (1986). Healing: A handbook for adult victims of sexual abuse. Minneapolis, MN: Author.

Childhelp USA (1988). Survivor's Guide. Los Angeles Child Help Center, P.O.Box 630, Hollywood, CA. 90028

Daugherty, L. B. (1984). Why me? Help for victims of child sexual abuse (Even if they are adults now). Racine, WI: Mother Courage Press.

Donaforte, L. (1982). I remembered myself: The journal of a survivor of childhood sexual abuse. Ukiah, CA.: author.

Evert, K. (1987). When you're ready: A woman's healing from physical and sexual abuse by her mother. Walnut Creek, CA: Launch Press.

Figley, C. R. (1985). Trauma and its wake: The study and treatment of post traumatic stress disorder. New York: Brunner/Mazel.

Finkelhor, D. (Ed.). (1986). A sourcebook on child sexual abuse. Beverly Hills, CA: Sage Publications.

Garbarino, J., Gutman, E, & Seeley, J. W. (1986). The psychologically battered child. San Francisco: Josey Bass.

Gelinas, D. J. (1983). The persisting negative effects of incest. Psychiatry, 46, 312-332.

Gil, E. (1984). Outgrowing the pain: A book for and about adults abused as children. Walnut Creek, CA: Launch Press.

Gravitz, H. L., & Bowden, J. D., (1985). Guide to recovery: A book for adult children of alcoholics. Holmes Beach, FL: Learning Publications.

Hay, Louise (1985). You can heal your life. Farmingdale, NY: Coleman

Helfer, R. E. (1978). Childhood comes first: A crash course in childhood. East Lansing, MI: Helfer

Kluft, R. P., (Ed.), (1985). Childhood antecedents of multiple personality. Washington, DC: American Psychiatric Press.

Kluft, R. (Ed.). (1985). Early antecedents of multiple personality.. New York: American Psychiatric Press.

Leehan, J., & Wilson, L. P. (1985). Grown-up abused children. Springfield, IL: Charles C. Thomas.

Lew, M. (1990). Victims no longer: Men recovering from incest and other sexual child abuse. New York: Harper and Row

Lindberg, F. H., & Distad, L. J. (1985). Post traumatic disorder women who experienced childhood incest. Child abuse and neglect, 9(3), 329-334.

Linn, M. & Linn, D. (1983). Healing life's hurts. Mahwah, NJ: Paulist Press.

Maltz, W. & Holman, B. (1986). Incest and Sexuality: A guide to understanding and healing. Lexington, MA: Lexington.

McConnell, P. (1986). A workbook for healing adult children of alcoholics. San Francisco, CA: Harper & Row.

Miller, A. (1983). For your own good. New York: Farrar Straus Giroux.

Morris, M. (1982). If I should die before I wake. New York: J.P. Tarcher.

Norwood, R. (1986). Women who love too much. New York: Pocket Books

Phelps, J.K., & Nourse, A.E. (1986). The hidden addiction. Boston, MA: Little, Brown.

Rolf, I.P. (1977). Rolfing: The integration of human structures. Santa Monica, CA: Dennis-Landman.

Rush, F. (1980). The best kept secret: Sexual abuse of children. Englewood Cliffs, NJ: Prentice-Hall.

Sexton, D. (1988). Vulnerable populations: Evaluation and treatment of suxually abused children and adult survivor. Lexington, MA: Lexington

Sgroi, S. (Ed.). (1988). Vulnerable populations: Evaluation and treatment of sexually abused children and adult survivor. Lexington, MA: Lexington.

Sisk, S. L., & Hoffman, C. F., (1987). Inside scars. Gainesville, FL: Pandora Press.

Van der Kolk, B. A., (Ed.), (1984). Post-traumatic stress disorder: Psychological and Biological Sequelae. Washington, DC: American Psychiatric Press.

Woititz, J.G. (1989). Healing your sexual self. Deerfield Beach, FL: Health Communications.

Wynne, C. E. (1986). That looks like a nice house. Walnut Creek, CA: Launch Press.